Nobility and Civility

Nobility & Civility

Asian Ideals of Leadership and the Common Good

Wm. Theodore de Bary

Harvard University Press   Cambridge, Massachusetts, and London, England   2004

Library of Congress Cataloging-in-Publication Data

De Bary, William Theodore, 1919–
    Nobility and civility : Asian ideals of leadership and the common good /
Wm. Theodore de Bary.
        p.   cm.
    Includes bibliographical references and index.
    ISBN 0-674-01557-6 (alk. paper)
    1. Leadership—Asia—History.   2. Civil society—Asia—History.
3. Leadership—Religious aspects—Confucianism.   4. Leadership—
Religious aspects—Hinduism.   5. Leadership—Religious aspects—
Buddhism.   I. Title.

JQ36.D43   2004
303.3'4'095—dc22   2004042212

For Fanny
First, last, and always
". . . verdantly still"

Contents

Preface

The nature of true leadership; its relation to learning, virtue, and education in human governance; the role in society of what today is often called the public intellectual—these have been questions for humankind in some form since the dawn of history and civilization. In one voice or another the prophet, the epic poet (once characterized by Mark Van Doren as "The Noble Voice"), and the early philosophers have spoken to this, as do the foundation myths of the classical traditions. What are the personal qualities that enable those in power—whether that power is inherited, seized by force, or perhaps won by some kind of election—to claim authority over others, or to gain their compliance with the ways of civilized life, free from violence, coercion, or deception?

Here we recognize the issue most broadly as one of civility, even if not in the form of a "civil society" as modern scholars have written about it. The latter concept does have relevance to how organized life can be sustained in the face of the unprecedented violence that dominates so much of contemporary life. Indeed, coping with institutionalized violence and sophisticated technologies requires systemic solutions; these features of society cannot be controlled simply by the charismatic force of noble individuals alone. But in early times the example of the truly noble leader was recognized as crucial to the restraint and containment of violence, insofar as that example spoke to the conscience of all, not just to the ruling elite.

If I use the word "conscience" here, regardless of how human consciousnesses may have differed from age to age and place to place, it is because in the midst of cultural differences these concerns are recognized also as constants in human life, and are in some sense shared—as indeed common "human" concerns. Confucius spoke of this self-awareness as a sense of shame or as its corollary, a sense of self-respect, to which the ruler, if he be truly a leader, must appeal if he is not to rely on coercive means that eventually undo themselves.

For Confucius this concept of true nobility and genuine leadership was a high calling. He did not underestimate the demands it laid on the educated person or man of learning who also bore the burden of leadership in society. In the *Analects,* he calls on the class of well-bred aristocrats known as *shi* in ancient China (somewhat like the knights or gentlemen of the medieval West) to put on the shining armor of moral virtue and public learning. It is said: "The *shi* must be stout-hearted and enduring, for his burden is heavy and his Way is long. Humaneness is the burden he takes upon himself. Is it not heavy? Only in death does his Way come to an end. Is it not long?" (*Analects* 8:7).

If today the concept of the public intellectual is upheld in contrast to the academician isolated in an ivory tower, we may draw some lessons, and possibly some inspiration, from the Asian ideals that survive, not as abstract ivory-tower ideals, but as having endured something of the long, conflicted struggle Confucius foresaw for the scholar "stout of heart" and "enduring" in the Way.

Although one may well question whether such ideals can be taken as universals or eternal verities, one may still recognize the cases cited here as inspired attempts to grapple with perennial issues or persistent human dilemmas, worthy of our consideration even now in their very conflicted contexts. The "globalization" much talked about today is a case in point. Most often it refers to the persistent trend toward the unification of the world economy and the homogenization of culture in response to a spreading technology. But the universalization of values and standards of culture has been a feature of expanding civilizations since the dawn of history, and the problems attendant upon it (as well as the response to these) offer a perspective on the dilemmas of our own era.

If modernization is not simply to mean the extension to other peoples, in an unquestioned and uncritical way, of current trends in the West, then the globalization of knowledge must take into account the values and experiences of other major civilizations. Today, unfortunately, these values are poorly understood even in their original settings or homelands, because of the long disruption of native traditions and the radical reorientation of the educated leadership to other immediate goals or European ideologies.

Generally speaking, such classic values have been known in modern times, if at all, through the revered classics and scriptures of major traditions, but their relevance and adaptability to modern circumstances remains unclear if these values are conceived simply in the abstract, without any understanding of the difficulties experienced historically in applying or practicing them. In other words, traditional values need to be understood as historically evolving, and in that process as marked by much ambiguity and contestation—contestation that has arisen especially in multicultural encounters, wherein ideals are almost always compromised by messy human complications. The Asian ideals discussed here are thus seen as conflicted human values, conflicted in the same sense as in my earlier book, *The Trouble with Confucianism.*

This book, which ranges widely over several civilizations and historical eras, can only be suggestive of how evolving concepts of leadership ("nobility") and public morality ("civility") in several Asian traditions may contribute to the humanizing of the current globalization process. It does not propose exact prescriptions for present problems, but may serve the purpose of general education in the face of the modern rush to find technical solutions, ready at hand but often oversimplified, to our current dilemmas. Without an awareness of people's past experience in the implementation of their own ideal values, it will be difficult to see how anyone could be expected to recognize and cope with similar problems in the present. And unless some such awareness becomes part of the education of all, one can expect that the globalizing process may well be degrading, dehumanizing, and destructive of the earth, beyond anything seen in the past.

My treatment of this theme includes reflections on the views expressed in classic texts of the major Asian traditions in India, China, and Japan. Obviously, my method is highly selective, and of relevant source materials, not at all exhaustive, but I have chosen to work with texts that are well known and either long respected or long contested in these traditions—ones that have often been referred to as landmarks of cultural history and in this sense survive today as relatively "hard" artifacts testifying to the continuities of civilized life.

Because these texts are widely recognized as classics or monumental works, they have readily attracted the attention of translators, and most of them exist in multiple renditions. Since I myself, however, have been the sponsor, editor, or translator of many texts prepared for use in Asian Civilizations or Humanities courses based on primary sources, I have most often relied on the translations available in the several volumes of *Sources of Indian, Chinese, Japanese* and *Korean Traditions* published by Columbia University Press.

In the process I have leapt from one civilization to another, generally following the progressive development of ideas within given traditions as they spread from India to East Asia, or within the latter from China to Japan and Korea. In doing so I have tried to deal cross-culturally with movements of thought as they encountered similar stages or challenges in other historical situations. This approach then does not always follow consecutive linear developments within a given history or culture, and I may not always have managed a smooth transition from one to another. If so, I apologize to readers who sometimes may be called upon to stretch their imaginations over too broad a span.

The subject of this book was also the subject of workshops and colloquia which I held with colleagues and students at Columbia in 2002–03, and what I have to say here reflects many beneficial exchanges with the members of those groups, especially Ryuichi Abe, Irene Bloom, Richard Bulliet, Hamid Dabashi, Kathy Eden, Julian Franklin, Mary McGee, James Mirollo, Andrew Nathan, Richard Norris, Peter Pouncey, Frances Pritchett, Wayne Proudfoot, George Saliba, Allan Silver, J. W. Smit, David Weiss-Halivni, and Neguin Yavari. In the preparation of the book I have been helped, as so often in the past, by Miwa Kai, Marianna Stiles, and Fanny Brett de Bary.

I wish to acknowledge the debt I owe to two anonymous readers for Harvard University Press, whose insightful comments and suggestions have brought significant improvements, I believe, to the presentation of my ideas.

I also wish to acknowledge the hospitality of the East-West Center, Honolulu, where much of the writing of this book was done in the winter of 2002–03. Special thanks to Elizabeth Buck, Charles Morrison, and Wendy Nohara.

Nobility and Civility

Confucius' Noble Person

When a leading Japanese proponent of liberal democracy, Yoshino Sakuzō, discussed the prospect for constitutional government in Japan in 1916, he prefaced his analysis of constitutional structures by pointing to the difference between formal enactments and the political culture needed to sustain them:

> Whether or not constitutional government will work well is partly a matter of structure and procedures, but it is also a question of the general level of the peoples' knowledge and virtue. . . . The fundamental prerequisite for perfecting constitutional government . . . is the cultivation of knowledge and virtue among the generality of the people. . . . (It is extremely important not to rely on politicians alone, but to make use of the cooperative efforts of educators, religious leaders, and thinkers in all areas of society.)
>
> The United States and Mexico illustrate how two countries with equally well-developed forms of constitutional government may be at opposite ends of the scale in its operation as a result of the different levels of knowledge and virtue allowed by their peoples.[1]

Here, in emphasizing that the level of political morality and an informed public are even more crucial to the
outcome than formal structures, Yoshino appears squarely
placed at a time in early twentieth century Japan when
civic mindedness on the part of the people as a whole, and
not just virtue ascribed to the leadership elite, had become
an issue as political democracy was advanced to replace an
earlier, more aristocratic and authoritarian political order.
But if he calls upon "educators, religious leaders and thinkers" to aid in this process of raising the level of the peoples' informed participation, it is to be understood that the
"knowledge and virtue" he talks about will necessarily involve a mix of received values and new ideas appropriate to
a modernizing situation.

In the Japanese case, the received values could be
summed up in terms of the basic Confucian ethic popular-
ized in the eighteenth and nineteenth centuries, as well as
the vestiges of a medieval samurai ethic that had come to
be identified as *bushidō* (The Way of the Warrior). The
Tokugawa shogunate had claimed that it brought the civil
and military virtues together in one stable order after centuries of medieval feudal warfare. Indeed, some ideologues
of the Meiji era had propagated the idea that the new
citizenry should combine the samurai ethic with learning from the West, incorporating something of the ideal values of the old aristocracy in the ethos of a general public
now assuming some share in the responsibilities of governance.

At the time he wrote, Yoshino's concern about the prevalence of attitudes prejudicial to the workings of civil constitutional government might well have referred to the
bushidō mentality and military extremists who were openly

opposed to the rule of political parties, and who in the 1930s did indeed attempt violent coups against party governments. Yet it is an indication of Yoshino's worries about preserving the integrity of parliamentary processes that he focused instead on the baneful influence of the new plutocracy—the corruption of money—rather than misguided samurai idealism.

Of the traditional ideals that Yoshino might have identified with "knowledge and virtue," certainly Confucianism is the most likely source of a civility (cultural refinement) combining intellectual and moral virtues. Well-known to Meiji period readers of the Neo-Confucian Four Books, from the Emperor Meiji himself down to newly educated commoners, were passages in the *Analects* such as this: "Lead them by means of regulations and keep order among them by punishments, and the people will evade them and lack any sense of shame. Lead them through virtue and the rites, and they will have a sense of shame and thus correct themselves" (*Analects* 2:3).

Here Confucius is addressing members of a vestigial ruling aristocracy and emphasizes the importance of consensual rule that depends on an appeal to people's self-respect and voluntary compliance with the law. "Virtue and the rites" sum up a moral culture that is conducive to governance based on voluntary compliance—a civility supportive of civilized rule. It implies, however, a concordance between the values of the leadership class—here represented by the Noble Person (*junzi*) whose moral stature and wisdom give real meaning and value to the *junzi* as a member of the hereditary aristocracy, at a time when that class was giving way to a more meritocratic bureaucracy (6th to 3rd c. BCE).

Another passage in the *Analects* underscores this consensual element based on shared moral values:

> Zigong asked about government. The Master said: "Sufficient food, sufficient arms, and the confidence of the people." Zigong said, "If one, unavoidably, had to dispense with one of these three, which of them should go first?" The Master said, "The arms." Zigong, "If one had to do without another, then what?" The Master said, "Do without the food. Since ancient times there has always been death, but without confidence a people cannot stand." (*Analects* 12:7)

The Chinese word *xin*, translated here as "confidence," can also be understood as "trust." In either case, a fiduciary concept of governance and a reliance on the civil arts *(wen)*, rather than the military *(wu)*, are indicated. A common value system is assumed between the leader and the led, but without necessarily equating the two roles. The leadership role is one that requires an education, training, and culture; a "breeding" that can be respected by the people but emulated only to a certain degree by those less culturally advantaged.

As a class, the leadership elite were spoken of in Confucius' time as *shi,* who combined both military and civil functions. In Japan, much later, this was equated with the samurai, and one can recognize some rough analogue here between Confucius' time and Yoshino's in the *shi*'s transition from a military to a more civil function. But Yoshino is talking about a new citizenship; Confucius is not. The philosopher's ideal of the Noble Person may be an inspiration to the common man, but it was not to be expected that the "people" would participate like citizens in the business of governance. Indeed, the demands on the leadership class were heightened precisely because they bore responsibility for the welfare of a people often unable to help themselves and dependent rather on an informed, disciplined, self-controlled leadership. Hence the *Analects* speaks of the heavy responsibility of the *shi,* understood as members of a leadership elite bearing a heavy burden of public service.

In its most general sense, the burden of humane service to society might be taken up by anyone; to this extent it may be seen as a universal value, and something of the kind was certainly understood by later generations of educated Confucians—Chinese, Koreans, and Japanese—down through the ages. Yet learning and education, which Confucius and his successors Mencius and Xunzi saw as essential to the fulfillment of the leadership responsibility, were not available to all. In fact, in many times and places education was a distinct privilege of the leisured classes, which is why the Confucians insisted so on the responsibilities toward the disadvantaged and uneducated that always attached to this privilege of the elite—*noblesse oblige,* as it would be called in the West.

If this condition attaches to the wider extension of learning to commoners ("knowledge and virtue" as Yoshino would want to see it in his new citizens), another reservation attaches to the second component, Confucius' characterization of "virtue and the rites" as the consensual elements of a civilized order. This traditional social ritual, proper to the *shi* class, was a vestige of the refined culture *(wen)* Confucius identified with the leadership elite. It gave defined form to the moral values that so bordered on the spiritual order as to be undefinable, immeasurable qualities, unless specified in some customary form certified by past experience. But what was definable as within the reach of the elite, with their aristocratic traditions, was often not accessible to or practicable for commoners. This left a question as to how much observance of the rites could be counted on in society as a whole. Some forms of civility would certainly be practiced widely on the base, local level of social intercourse, but how relevant these social norms would be to any political process is another matter.

The two levels on which civil morality and the public interest might be understood in classical Confucianism are indicated in the text of Mencius. On the one hand, he, like others of his time, recognized the need for a distinct, educated leadership class, freed of manual labor so it could attend to the business of government. On the other hand, the qualifications of this class were identified by Mencius in terms of the "ranks of man" and the "ranks of Heaven." "The ranks of duke, minister, or high official are the nobility of man." "Humaneness, rightness, loyalty and trustworthiness are the nobility of Heaven" (Mencius 6A:16). Ideally, those holding the ranks of man (the leadership elite) would also exemplify the nobility of Heaven, but ideally, too, the nobility of Heaven was represented by moral values that any man could emulate.

This convergence of the two sets of values is also indicated in Mencius' ideal of the local community as modeled by the well-field system. Here fields were to be divided equally among families working the land (spoken of as representing the "private interest"), while they shared in the working of the "public" (gong) land to support the governing authority. The word gong here is the same as that for "duke" in the "ranks of man"; thus this concept of social or political authority (rank) converged with a concept of the public good, with no discontinuity between the true nobility of the leader and the values of civil morality incumbent on all. Yet as a practical matter, the question remained as to how well or in what way either the leadership or the led could measure up to these standards.

In classical Confucianism the moral ground on which both the leadership and the people stood was the family virtues shared by all orders of society, rulers and subjects alike. This is exemplified in the founding myth of a civilized order established by the sage-king Yao, whose civil virtues contrast with the martial prowess of most dynastic founders.

> Examining into antiquity, we find that the Emperor Yao was called Fangxun. He was reverent, intelligent, accomplished, sincere, and mild. He was sincerely respectful and capable of modesty. His light covered the four extremities of the empire and extended to Heaven above and the Earth below. He was able to make bright his great virtue and bring affection to the nine branches of the family. When the nine branches of the family had become harmonious, he distinguished and honored the hundred clans. When the hundred clans had become illustrious, he harmonized the myriad states. The numerous people were amply nourished and prosperous and became harmonious.[2]

Here the civil virtues and family values are one, as the gentle charisma of the paterfamilias radiates out to concentric circles of kinship so that all humankind unites in the bonds of family affection. This image is equally true of the founding myth in the Indian epic *Ramayana*, where the ideal king is also the loving father of his people, and the bonds of family relationship—filiality and brotherliness especially—provide the basis of a "constitutional" dynastic succession and political due process.

What is striking in the Chinese case is that within the
scope of the Confucian classics we find a chronicle that
goes one step beyond this conception of an ideal society
constituted on the nobility of family-style leadership to
something like a civil society expressed in the Confucian
(and more particularly Mencian) conception of the Noble
Person as the loyal minister whose prime virtue consists in
his honest, forthright correction of the ruler. As this virtue
and function are rendered in the Confucian *Chronicle of
Mr. Zuo* (4th to 3rd c. BCE), a civil process, still predicated
on the family ideal, goes on to involve all classes and levels
of society in the function of mutual remonstrations and ref-
ormation. In the *Chronicle*'s account, Duke Dao of Jin dis-
cusses with Shi Kuang, or Music Master Kuang, the forced
abdication of Duke Xian, ruler of the neighboring state of
Wei. Duke Xian had been driven out of his domain in 550
BCE as a result of his misrule. Shi Kuang uses the opportunity to speak of the love and concern of Heaven for the
common people and to underscore the responsibility of a
ruler to devote himself to their well-being and, especially, to
heed the remonstrations of his ministers. In this case, however, all levels of society, down to the very lowest, are seen
as participating in the process of admonition. Particularly
striking is the inclusion of artisans, blind musicians, merchants, and commoners in this picture of a participatory
process that does not restrict the counseling function only
to the elite.

Duke Xiang, Fourteenth year (550 BCE)
Shi Kuang was attending the ruler of Jin. The latter said,
"The people of Wei have driven out their ruler—what a ter-
rible thing!"

Shi Kuang replied, "Perhaps it was the ruler himself who did terrible things. When a good ruler goes about rewarding good and punishing excess, he nourishes his people as if they were his children, shelters them like Heaven, accommodates them like the earth. And when the people serve their ruler, they love him as they do their parents, look up to him like the sun and moon, revere him like the all-seeing spirits, fear him like thunder. How could they drive him out?

"The ruler is host to the spirits and the hope of the people. But if he exhausts the people's livelihood, deprives the spirits, skimps in the sacrifices to them, and betrays the hopes of the populace, then he ceases to be the host of the nation's altars of the soil and grain, and what use is he? What can one do but expel him?

"Heaven gave birth to the people and set up rulers to superintend and shepherd them and see to it that they do not lose their true nature as human beings. And because there are rulers, it provides helpers for them who would teach and protect them and see that they do not overstep the bounds. Hence the Son of Heaven has his chief officers, the feudal lords have their ministers, the ministers set up their collateral houses, gentlemen have their friends and companions, and the commoners, artisans, merchants, lackeys, shepherds, and grooms all have their relatives and close associates who help and assist them. If one does good they praise him, if he errs they correct him, if he is in distress they rescue him, if he is lost they restore him.

"Thus from the sovereign on down, each has his father or elder brother, his son or younger brother to assist and scrutinize his ways of management. The historians compile their documents, the blind musicians compose poems, the musicians chant admonitions and remonstrances, the high officials deliver words of correction, the gentlemen pass along remarks, the commoners criticize, the merchants voice their opinions in the market, and the hundred artisans contribute through their skills.

"Hence the 'Document of Xia' says: 'The herald with his wooden-clappered bell goes about the roads saying, "Let the officials and teachers correct the ruler, let the artisans pursue their skills and thereby offer remonstrance."'[3] In the first month, the beginning month of spring, this was done so that people might remonstrate against departures from the norm.

"Heaven's love for the people is very great. Would it then allow one man to preside over them in an arrogant and willful manner, indulging his excesses and casting aside the nature Heaven and Earth allotted them? Surely it would not!"[4]

What the *Chronicle* portrays here is not an egalitarian or democratic society, but nevertheless one in which all elements partake in the function of speaking for Heaven as the over-arching guardian and guarantor of the public sphere, the "sacred canopy" which the Confucians invoked by the saying: "Heaven does not speak; it speaks as my people speak."

Confucian texts often cite historical incidents as a pretext for the projection of ideal models, and the latter as the basis for a critique of the existing order; thus the *Chronicle* has been understood traditionally to report actual events that illustrate moral principles. There may be some plausibility then to the charge, alleged in a later historical account of the founding of the first Imperial dynasty, the Qin (Ch'in), that Confucians engaged in open political criticism and dissent in the late Zhou period. Here the Confucians appear to be not only the elite custodians of a traditional ideal invoked to expose and condemn existing practices, but a group having the kind of rapport with the people at large that enables them to speak for the public and stir up trouble. In a memorial to the founder of the Qin Dynasty, the prime minister, Li Si, urges him to suppress the classic writings of Confucian critics who arouse popular dissent and disaffection:

In earlier times the empire disintegrated and fell into disorder, and no one was capable of unifying it. Thereupon the various feudal lords rose to power. In their discourses they all praised the past in order to disparage the present and embellished empty words to confuse the truth. Everyone cherished his own favorite school of learning and criticized what had been instituted by the authorities. But at present Your Majesty possesses a unified empire, has regulated the distinctions of black and white, and has firmly established for yourself a position of sole supremacy. And yet these independent schools, joining with each other, criticize the codes of laws and instructions. Hearing of the promulgation of a decree, they criticize it, each from the standpoint of his own school. At home they disapprove of it in their hearts; going out they criticize it in the thoroughfares. They seek a reputation by discrediting their sovereign; they appear superior by expressing contrary views, and they lead the lowly multitude in the spreading of slander. If such license is not prohibited, the sovereign power will decline above and partisan factions will form below. It would be well to prohibit this.

Your servant suggests that all books in the imperial archives, save the memoirs of Qin, be burned. All persons in the empire, (except for members of the State Academy of Learned Scholars), who are in possession of the *Classic of Odes,* the *Classic of Documents* and discourses of the hundred philosophers should take them to the local governors and have them indiscriminately burned. Those who dare to talk to each other about the *Odes* and *Documents* should be executed and their bodies exposed in the marketplace. Anyone referring to the past to criticize the present should, together with all members of his family, be put to death.[5]

This testimony from a critic of the Confucians would suggest that not only the minister-counselor as Noble Person, but the common people (even the most handicapped) were speaking out on behalf of the common public interest. Apparently they were not so preoccupied with their own family affairs and interests that they could not take on the role and risks of instigating civil discussion and debate—challenging enough in this case to invite repression from a ruling power bent on monopolizing the public sphere.

In the following chapter we go on to ask whether something similar to this Chinese nobility, civility, and civil discourse is to be found in the early texts of the emerging Indian civilization.

2

The Noble Paths of
Buddha and Rama

India of the so-called Axial Age had two comparable if also competing examples of an ideal of nobility, originally identified with a leadership elite, but later generalized, to a greater or lesser degree, as a value appropriate to all. To illustrate the point in relation to Buddhism I shall draw on the *Dhammapada,* a standard work of the Theravada Buddhist tradition, and in regard to Hinduism, the epic *Ramayana* in the classic version of Valmiki (7th c. BCE?). Both examples assume a similar social background characterized by the coexistence (often competing) of a religious elite identified with a Brahmin class (claiming higher authority), and a political class identified with a ruling aristocracy, the *kshatriya,* originally a military aristocracy.

In these works the claims of both classes are called into question and new ideals are put forward—a rough parallel to the re-evaluation by Confucius and Mencius of the role of the nobleman *(junzi)* from a hereditary aristocrat (Mencius' "ranks of man") to the *junzi* as the moral ideal of the Noble Person (exemplifying the "nobility of Heaven").

In the *Dhammapada* the focus is on the way of life of the

arhat (monk), the practitioner of the Noble Eightfold Path laid out by the Buddha on the basis of the principles contained in the Four Noble Truths. "Noble" here reflects the aristocratic calling of the *kshatriya* class from which the Buddha comes, but it is given new meaning in fulfillment of the legendary prediction (at his birth) that Shakyamuni (Siddhartha Gautama, 6th c. BCE) would abandon his princely inheritance and secular power to pursue a spiritual mastery beyond the worldly order. Nobility here represents an ideal of lofty spiritual emancipation, characterized by self-control, equanimity, and dedication to a religious goal: the attainment of Nirvana through sustained meditative practice. It is predicated on a recognition of the impermanence and insubstantiality of all things, concepts, and values—even ordinary moral, social, or cultural goods—with which individuals normally identified their selfhood, thereby propping up an illusory sense of a substantial, enduring self, where in fact none such existed.

This goal was to be achieved through individual effort, and while its practice might be enhanced through association with a religious community of like-minded individuals, it was not concerned with the political or social order as such. The Buddha had left the palace and did not return to the exercise of temporal power or the reform of organized society, both of which might prove to be only illusory goals.

The concept of nobility as superior to political power or social rank is clearly set forth in the *Dhammapada,* where spiritual attainment is spoken of as:

> *Better than sole sovereignty over the earth*
> *Or the journey to heaven,*
> *Than lordship over all the world.*[1]

redeemable by the Covenant; instead, the world and its creatures are seen as eternal—undergoing constant generation, degeneration, and regeneration in an endless cycle. (Curiously, however, the process is abetted by an Evil One, of whom it is said that, after tasting the earth "he became filled with the savour of the earth and craving entered into him. Other beings, following his example, tasted the savoury earth and . . . craving entered into them"—a way of identifying craving as a central concern of Buddhism [105]).

Eventually this general craving led to acquisitiveness and to competition for the means of its satisfaction, then to stealing, lying, and other evils that called for punishment. Out of this turmoil arose the need for a ruler: someone who would "be angry when indignation is called for, who would censure whatever should be censured, and should banish anyone who deserves to be banished." On this basis rulers appeared as well as the ruling class of warriors known as kshatriya, from which the Buddha himself had emerged. It is a particular point of this so-called Buddhist Book of Genesis, characterized by the translator as "dealing with the evolution of government," that the warrior class has priority over the religious order.

The religious men, according to this version, had tried to deal with human evil and immorality by withdrawing from society and practicing meditation, but failing in this, returned to villages and towns "to make books" and thus become professional scripture scholars rather than practitioners of meditation. Interestingly, the text says of these brahmans, "at that time they were looked on as the lowest, although now they are thought the best" (111).

Clearly, this genesis story serves the purpose of putting

One who attains this heroic ideal surpasses those traditionally identified with leadership roles in Vedic society, the aristocrat and the priest:

A bull, splendid, heroic
A great sage, a victor
Passionless, one who has bathed, awakened
That one I call a brāhmana.(414)

Here the *arhat* who has succeeded in attaining Nirvana is clothed in all the epic attributes of the warrior class—a "bull," a "victor," but also a sage (a quality attainable by both wise rulers and Brahmin priests).

In the *Dhammapada* the traditional Indian model of religious virtue, the *brāhmana*, is reconceived as distinct from hereditary status, whether military/political or religious (either sacerdotal or ascetic):

Not by matted hair or by clan
Or by birth does one become a brāhmana
In whom is truth and dhamma,
He is the pure one, he is the brāhmana. (398)

And I do not call one a brāhmana
Merely by being born from a womb,
Sprung from a [brāhmana] mother
He is merely a bho-sayer. (399)

A "*bho*-sayer" is someone identified with the conventional politeness of a well-bred member of his hereditary class or caste. Here the *Dhammapada* is asserting a nobility that goes beyond mere good-breeding or gentility—a distinction that will become increasingly relevant and critical in all those Asian contexts in which personal nobility, social gentility, and even aesthetic sensibility are competing values among the leadership elite—as they become again, of course, in modern times with a modern citizenry hoping to achieve a multicultural civility.

The idea of nobility in early Buddhism focused on the heroic spiritual achievement of the Buddha and those who followed him; in this sense it was exceptional, but there was nothing exclusive about it or elitist in the social sense. Religious liberation was open to all. What made it appear later to be exclusive or elitist was, rather, the need in practice for some degree of seclusion for disciplined meditation—something practicable only for a few, who were supported in this special pursuit by the alms of the many, themselves laymen.

The grounds for this are already evident in the *Dhammapada*'s characterization of the *arhat* or *bhikkhu*:

> *One who wears rags from a dust heap*
> *Lean, having veins [visibly] spread over all his body*
> *Meditating alone in the forest,*
> *That one I call a brāhmana. (399)*

> *Few are those among humans*
> *The people who reach the shore beyond. (169)*

The isolation demanded for concentrated practice also calls for detachment from ordinary society:

> *Having forsaken a shadowy* dhamma
> *The wise-one would cultivate the bright,*
> *Having come from familiar abode to no-abode*
> *In disengagement hard to relish. (170)*

Nevertheless there is a place for fellow aspirants, and a reason for religious orders sharing a monastic life:

> *Let one not associate with low persons, bad friends*
> *But let one associate with noble persons, worthy friends.*
>   (162)

In time this nobility as a spiritual idea or monastic or came to be perceived as elitist, for the privileged few. WI Buddhism divided into two principal branches, in the l Mahayana view of what its followers called the Hinay the "Small Vehicle," the monks so privileged were als littled as proud—even though pride, self-satisfaction o clusiveness had no place at all in the original teaching

It must be said too that the qualities said to mar ideal behavior of the *bhikkhu* or *arhat* were by no n ones limited to an elite: restraint of the passions; sel trol and temperance in all things; equanimity in the { trial and suffering; friendliness and generosity in c with others; peaceableness and nonviolence (373– all of these were qualities that might grace humank any level of society or in any social position.

This view of the matter is supported by an accoun in the *Aganna Sutta* of the Pali canon, which the tr; has entitled "A Genesis Story."[2] Actually, the story centrally concerned with the origins of the Indi structure but explains this within a quasi-naturali ception of how the human condition developed appetites, desire, and craving produced by conta scum that formed on the face of the earth, and tasting of its savor by beings who had somehow f; a paradisal state of pure radiance.

This genesis is not an act of creation (as in the ment Genesis) by a God who affirms his creati pecially man as originally good, and even after

down the established religious elite, but having done so by attributing its failure to a falling away from the practice of meditation, the text goes on to show how a *kshatriya* "went from home into the homeless life saying 'I will be an ascetic.' Some *brahmans* did the same; likewise some *vaisyas* [tradesmen] and some *sudras* [laborers]. . . . Out of these four groups the company of ascetics came into being. Their origin was from just these beings like unto themselves, not different" (112). In other words, the "origin" explained here is that of the "ascetics," Buddhist monks who, irrespective of class, have left home to take up a life of meditation which the Brahmans had given up to become pundits and pedants.

For all the special pleading here on behalf of the Buddhist cause versus the established brahmanical religion, the story can be helpful in judging both the plausibility and tendentiousness of later Mahayana aspersions on the so-called Smaller Vehicle (Hinayana)—that it is somehow self-absorbed, exclusive, and elitist. A main point of the present account is that the true religious life is identified primarily, and primordially, with meditation, a practice and a state that anyone of any class can aspire to. In this case Theravada Buddhism presents itself as egalitarian and open to all.

At the same time, the religious practice itself, if not selfish, is nevertheless spoken of in this text as aimed at "winning" or "attaining one's own salvation" (104, 112); and the individuals who are said to have emerged from any of the four classes to become a *bhikkhu* or an *arhat* are repeatedly characterized as "ascetics meditating alone." Thus the religious life is egalitarian and classless in regard to its social antecedents and accessibility for all, but its practice is definitely demanding and strict enough so that not all, and perhaps only a few, will succeed in reaching the goal by that means.

To the extent that self-discipline and meditative praxis are necessarily, or at least to some extent, self-centered, one can recognize in the religious life of the ascetic or monk both the virtues and limitations of a path so focused on self-restraint, self-control, and intense self-concentration. Indeed, it is this element of self-control (though differently practiced) that can be seen as the shared ground of Buddhism and the Hinduism represented in our next prime text, the *Ramayana*.

Moreover, while recognizing how any teaching of self-restraint and self-control could contribute to civil conduct and a nonviolent solution to human conflicts, we also note that rulership and governance are seen here as essentially regulatory and punitive, and thus second-best as a way of dealing with human evil. Governance is of a worldly order from which one must be saved by a religion which transcends the ceaseless round of craving, illusion, and suffering, in the inexorable course of which no civil order or commonweal appears, nor is any public philosophy projected— only a recycling of the state of primordial radiance followed by another lapse into craving and suffering.

No doubt it was the pertinence of Buddhism's more positive spiritual values to the maintenance of peace and order in his or any society that led Ashoka (268–233 BCE), the third ruler of the Maurya dynasty, to encourage their adoption among his subjects, as proclaimed through the famous Pillar Edicts which he promulgated after his own violent conquest of Kalinga. These edicts called for obedience to parents and teachers, respect for the aged, and kindness to the poor and lowly. In addition, Ashoka stressed obedience to law and Buddhist righteousness, including "the law against killing certain animals." But the greatest progress of Righteousness, he said, comes from exhortation in favor of "no injury to life and abstention from killing living beings."[3]

Along with these peaceable professions, however, Ashoka made it clear that contrition for his own past resort to violence would not keep him from strict enforcement of his dictates. He warned any who might resist him that "there is power even in the remorse of the Beloved of the Gods [Ashoka]." He tells them to reform, "lest they be killed"(52).

In the end Ashoka's noble professions of the rule of Righteousness had little lasting effect. The distinguished historian of India, A. L. Basham, concluded that Ashoka's hope "that aggressive wars would cease forever as a result of his propaganda, was unfulfilled, and the successors of Ashoka seem to have been if anything even more militant than their predecessors. "It would seem, that Buddhism had little effect on encouraging peace within the borders of India" (47, quoting Basham).

"In fact," says Basham, "Buddhism had little direct effect on the political order . . . and its leaders seem often to have been rather submissive to temporal authority. An Erastian [i.e. accommodative] relationship between church and state is indicated in the inscriptions of Ashoka, and in Buddhist Ceylon the same relationship usually existed"(47). Indeed, the same could be said about Nepal, once part of the homeland of Buddhism, as well as countries like Thailand and Cambodia, where Buddhism has stood for centuries as the official religion but the political ideology has been for the most part derived from Hindu traditions.

A similar conclusion concerning Ashoka's Pillar Edicts is drawn in the more recent study of Donald K. Swearer. The teachings of the Edicts, which he calls Rock Edicts,

present an idealistic, humanitarian philosophy with few Buddhist doctrinal interests. Ashoka advocates docility to parents, liberality to friends, economy in expenditures and avoidance of disputes (rock edict 3). He urges self-mastery, purity of heart, gratitude, and fidelity (rock edict 7). Like the *Sigālaka Sutta*, a treatise on lay ethics to which the *dharma* of the rock edicts is sometimes compared, Ashoka advises right conduct toward servants, honor toward teachers, liberality to brahmans and recluses, and self-restraint toward all living things (rock edicts 9 and 11). His moral advice is inspiring but not specifically Buddhist.[4]

The legend of Ashoka as ideal Buddhist ruler *(chakravartin)* inspired rulers of Southeast Asia "to follow Ashoka's example of contributing lavishly to the monastic order" (67). Moreover, because "Buddhist monarchs of Southeast Asia enshrined Buddha relics in *stūpas* . . . they came to represent a magical or supernatural center for the kingdom" (72). In this process of bringing religious symbols and institutions into the kingly fold, the conception of the Buddhist universal ruler became fused with the god-king *(deva-rāja)* of Hinduism—a conception which finds impressive articulation in the great royal monuments of Angkor Wat (Cambodia), Pagan (Burma), and Sukhothai (Thailand). In these grand temple structures, the melding of the concepts of the god-king with the Buddha-king provided the basis for the assertion that "it was the king who was the great god of ancient [Buddhist] Cambodia, the one to whom the biggest groups of monuments and all the temples in the form of monuments were dedicated" (76, quoting George Coedes).

Contributing to the elevation of the ruler was the aforementioned cult of the relics of the Buddha, based on the belief in the "sacred power associated with the person of the Buddha. . . . The Buddha as consecrator of the land plays a central role; that is the Buddha's physical presence serves to establish a holy land" (92).

The foregoing outline suggests that, at the very least, there has been little problem historically in the adaptation of Buddhist concepts of spiritual nobility to the kind of civil ethos and political morality already prevalent in countries at one time or another influenced by Buddhism. In other words, the latter easily found common ground with existing political cultures and readily adapted to them.

This outcome points to an alternative concept of nobility that has proved more enduring in much of South Asia. Although appearing in many institutional and ritual forms, its most dramatic expression is found in the epic literature of the *Mahabharata* and the *Ramayana*. Taken together, these two epics narrate and dilate upon a range of grand themes and value-issues that arise when traditional societies emerge from a tribal or feudal aristocratic stage to an urban civilization with a new self-consciousness and sense of individual responsibility for the social, or even the cosmic, order. Thus the struggles of the epic hero characteristically reflect the conflict between the claims of family, clan, and tribe and the values of an emerging urban civilization, membership in which calls for more universal values transcending tribal and clan loyalties.

We have already seen how early Buddhism challenged these same established values. To take up the religious life was to "leave home and household"; the Buddhist discipline of the Noble Eightfold Path challenged both the ways of the Brahmans (ritual and ascetic) and the ways of the warrior nobility whose prime role was the exercise of power. The *Mahabharata* (4th c. BCE to 4th c. CE) and *Ramayana* speak to the same issues but in ways that, while critical of those who claim to represent the established social order of *brahman* and *kshatriya,* nevertheless attempt to fulfill traditional values and rituals in a new way, without denying the world of human values (in other words, without aiming at the "other shore" of Nirvana and transcendence of ordinary experience), but carrying these natural, human values to a higher level.

Both the *Mahabharata* and the *Ramayana,* as epic poetry, speak with the Noble Voice that is characteristic of epic as a genre,[5] and they both speak to the crisis of a nobility (the *kshatriya*) that must now express itself in terms that go beyond kinship relations. Though the *Mahabharata* is well known for its varied, encyclopedic content, its compendious coverage of a broad range of themes—military, social, moral, and religious—it is best known for a separate chapter, "The Bhagavad Gita," which features the moral dilemma and attendant pathological crisis of the warrior Arjuna.

On the field of battle, in what is an internecine war within the ruling class, Arjuna experiences a conflict over whether he should fight and slay his own kinsmen. It is a paralyzing contradiction for one whose highest concepts of duty are bound up with the kinship system. How can one perform one's traditional duty, if to defend kinship values involves destroying one's kin? (In modern terms one recognizes this as the crisis faced by J. Robert Oppenheimer in creating and using the atomic bomb: how can one, in defense of civilization, build a weapon that may destroy civilization?) Arjuna is finally persuaded by his charioteer Krishna, an avatar of the god Vishnu, that he must go ahead and fulfill his caste duty to fight and kill, while "renouncing the fruits of his action," offering them as a sacrifice to the Supreme Lord. Thus the Gita confirms the traditional role of the warrior class, but invests it with a new religious significance—action performed on a higher spiritual plane, transcending the conflict and contradiction in human moral sentiments. Nobility is not denied or rejected as a concept of leadership in the human order, but it is seen as viable only in the light of one's recognition and acceptance of a higher cosmic order and overarching religious conception.

Like the *Mahabharata*, the *Ramayana* presents a vast panorama of epic human conflicts. The two are also alike in that the main focus is on the heroic role of the *kshatriya* as the warrior/ruler class, that is, they raise the issue again of what is true nobility. In much of the epic Rama performs as a heroic warrior on behalf of righteousness, but early on a crucial scene involves the due consecration of Rama as successor to his father's kingship. The context again is one of the traditional kinship system, and the consecration ritual serves to ratify legitimate succession to rulership in a dynastic system, lest a power struggle break out between rival claimants within the ruling house. Although, as the story is told, this succession has overwhelming popular approval, one of the king's wives, Kaikeyi, asks him, in fulfillment of an earlier open-ended promise, not to go ahead with the consecration of Rama but instead to install her own son Bharata (and Rama's half-brother) as heir apparent. At this the king is in utter conflict as between his own preference for Rama (which is that of the people too, and even of Bharata himself, whose character combines fraternal virtue and family solidarity) on the one hand, and on the other hand, the need to fulfill his earlier promise—to be true to his word. In the end the king keeps his word, and Rama is sent into exile while his brother is enthroned as king. No one, not even the brother, is in favor of this, but Rama accepts it, despite repeated entreaties from all sides, including Bharata, that Rama claim his rightful inheritance in disregard of the king's decision to fulfill this earlier misbegotten promise to Kaikeyi. Rama goes into exile in the forest.

In Rama's case the conflict arises from the evil doings of one scheming woman. It is not a struggle among Rama's kin. Rama himself, his brother, and members of the family exemplify throughout the utmost in familial loyalty and affection. Everything hinges rather on Rama's sole insistence on being true to one's given word—whether his father's to his wife or his to his father. No sentimental concerns, no extenuating circumstances or countervailing prudential advice could be allowed to vitiate this fundamental principle: that anyone qualified to rule (whether Rama or indeed his father) must be, above all, trustworthy in regard to his given word. As Valmiki tells the story, vividly dramatizing the passions and insidious scheming of Kaikeyi, as well as the misery of a king brought low by his own weakness of will, Rama stands heroically steadfast in his determination to do what is right.

As the *Ramayana* portrays it, trust between ruler and ruled is the foundation not only of civilized society but of the whole cosmic order (its reliability, dependability) with which human governance must be coordinate. Failure to

keep one's given word, regardless of all extenuating circumstances and convenient excuses, rends the fabric of trust
that is not only the basis of fiduciary governance but the basis of the whole natural and celestial order.

Closely allied to this conception of duty is Rama's act of
self-renunciation. This is not renunciation of the world in
the manner of the Buddha Shakyamuni, who gave up kingship as offering no remedy to the problem of human suffering and illusion. Rama eventually, after fourteen years of
exile, returns to rule as a true king, but in the meantime he
has demonstrated that only one ready to renounce power is
truly qualified to exercise it. The point of the story is that
virtuous rule remains a value, while true nobility is raised
to a plane higher than simply the exemplification of family
obligations. True nobility means being true to oneself, not
just good and loyal to one's kin.

The absoluteness of this claim is underscored by the
Ramayana's relativizing of the status of both the warrior
and priestly classes. The author does not challenge the
caste system as such, nor does he question monarchial
rule, but his account of the matter subjects these to a
higher law of moral accountability. The point is most clearly
made in a crucial encounter between Rama and "a prominent Brahman" named Jabali, who tries to deflect Rama
from his chosen course, addressing him precisely in terms
of what it means to be a noble man. Jabali's argument starts
off like a parody of Buddhist skepticism and antinomianism; then it quickly shifts to grounds of expediency based
on a self-indulgent hedonism—a direct challenge to the
values of the kinship system and the traditional ritual order.
In Rama's response to Jabali, however, even the accepted
"code of the *kshatriya*" is belittled as "ignoble."

Valmiki's passage dealing with this telling encounter expresses most eloquently the whole morality of the *Ramayana,* which warrants quoting it at some length.

Sarga 100

1. As righteous Rāma was consoling Bharata, a prominent brahman named Jābāli addressed him in words at variance with righteousness;
2. "Come now, Rāghava, [i.e. Rama] you must not entertain such nonsensical ideas like the commonest of men, and you a noble-minded man in distress.
3. "What man is kin to anyone, what profit has anyone in anyone else? A person is born alone, and all alone he must die.
4. "And thus, Rāma, the man who feels attachment thinking, 'This is my mother, this my father,' should be regarded as a madman, for in truth no one belongs to anyone.
5–6. "A man traveling from village to village will spend the night somewhere and next day leave the place where he stopped and continue on—in the same way, Kākutstha, his father and mother, his home and wealth are mere stopping places for a man. The wise feel no attachment to them.
7. "You must not, best of men, abdicate the kingship of your fathers and embark upon this unwise course, painful, rocky, and full of thorns.
8. "Consecrate yourself in prosperous Ayodhyā; the city is waiting for you, wearing her single braid of hair.
9. "Indulge in priceless royal pleasures and enjoy yourself in Ayodhyā, prince, like Śakra in his heaven.
10. "Daśaratha was nobody to you, and you were nobody to him. The king was one person, you another, So do as I am urging.
11. "The King has gone where he had to go; such is the

course all mortals follow. You are merely deluding yourself.

12. "The men I grieve for, and I grieve for no one else, are all who place 'righteousness' above what brings them profit. They find only sorrow in this world, and at death their lot is annihilation just the same.

13. "People here busy themselves because 'It is the Eighth Day, the rite for the ancestors.' But just look at the waste of food—what really is a dead man going to eat?

15. "It was only as a charm to secure themselves donations that cunning men composed those books that tell us, 'Sacrifice, give alms, sanctify yourself, practice asceticism, renounce.'

16. "Accept the idea once and for all, high-minded prince, that there exists no world to come. Address yourself to what can be perceived and turn your back on what cannot.

17. "Give precedence to these ideas of the wise, with which the whole world concurs. Be appeased by Bharata and accept the kingship."

Sarga 101

1. Upon hearing Jābāli's words, Rāma, the most truthful of men, replied with sound argument, his own convictions quite unshaken:

2. "What you have said in the hopes of pleasing me is wrong with only a semblance of right; it is harm that simulates help.

3. "A person wins no esteem among the wise when his conduct belies his tenets, and he acts in evil ways, recognizing no bounds.

4. "It is conduct alone that proclaims whether a man is highborn or base, honest or dishonest, brave or merely a braggart.

5–6. "It would be ignobility with a semblance of nobility, dishonesty with an outward show of honesty, dishonor masquerading as honor, indecency disguised as decency, were I to reject the good and accept such unrighteousness. For it merely wears the cloak of righteousness;

7. "What sensible man anywhere in the world, aware of what is right and wrong, would hold me in high esteem—a man of evil acts, a corruptor of the world?

8. "To whose actions should I be conforming, and how then should I reach heaven, were I to adopt this practice and break my promise?

9. "Besides, the entire world would follow suit in acting as it pleases, for subjects will behave just like their king.

10. "The actions of a king must always be truthful and benevolent. The kingdom will thereby be true, the world firmly established on truth.

11. "It is truth and truth alone that both gods and seers hold in esteem, for the man who tells the truth in this world will attain the highest abode.

12. "As from a serpent do people recoil from a man who speaks falsely. Truth, it is said, is the ultimate form of righteousness in this world, and the very root of heaven.

13. "Truth is the lord of this world, the goddess of the lotus resides in truth, all things are rooted in truth, there is no higher goal than truth.

14. "The giving of alms, sacrifices, the offering of oblations, the practice of asceticism, and the *vedas* themselves are based on truth, and so it is truth that must be one's highest aim.

15. "One man protects the world, one protects his house; one is exalted in heaven, and one sinks down to hell.

16. "As for me, why should I not truthfully follow my father's command? I have always been true to my word, and I have pledged upon my truth.

19. "This personal code of righteousness I know myself to be the true one. Wise men have always borne the burden it imposes, and I gladly accept it.

20. "I reject the *kshatriya*'s code, where unrighteousness and righteousness go hand in hand, a code that only debased, vicious, covetous, and evil men observe.

21. "And sinful action is of three sorts: One can have evil thoughts, or do an evil deed, or tell a lie.

22. "Land, fame, glory and wealth seek out the man who holds to truth and ever attend on him. Let a man then devote himself to truth alone.

23. "What you consider the best course is in fact ignoble; the statements you make urging me to 'do what is good for me' are mere sophistry.

24. "I have promised my guru to live in the forest. How then can I do as Bharata bids, and defy the bidding of my guru?

25. "I made a promise in the presence of my guru—it brought delight to the heart of Queen Kaikeyī—and that promise shall not be broken.

26–27. "I will thus live a life of purity in the forest, restricting my food to holy things, roots, fruit, and flowers, and satisfying the gods and ancestors. My five senses will have contentment enough and I shall be maintaining the world on its course. Moreover, I myself shall remain a sincere believer, fully aware of what is right and what is wrong.

30. "Truthfulness, righteousness, and strenuous effort, compassion for creatures and kindly words, reverence for *brahmans,* gods, and guests is the path, say the wise, to the highest heaven.

31. "Those men who are earnest in righteousness and keep company with the wise, who are supremely generous, nonviolent, and free from taint, those supreme and

mighty sages are the ones truly worthy of reverence in this world."[6]

The foregoing by no means exhausts the heroic virtues of Rama celebrated in the *Ramayana,* which include the traditional ideals of the righteous warrior in battle, the dutiful son, loving husband, loyal brother, and so on, but if, at the outset of his work, Valmiki suggests that Rama is the model of perfect virtue, it remains true that all of these other roles and corresponding virtues are qualified by Rama's sense of a supreme duty as king and upholder of the moral order. All these other duties or obligations—even his devotion to his wife, Sita—are subject to his kingly responsibility. His own beloved, his family, even his royal throne, may be set aside, if need be, in favor of his royal duty to sustain the right. But, whatever the sacrifice, in the end his path of duty is one of world affirmation, not world renunciation.

It is this ideal of total, self-renouncing duty that has given the *Ramayana* such wide human currency, far beyond its Indian birthplace. Whatever his other virtues, and however idealized or even deified Rama became in the popular devotional cults that emerged from the Rama legend, it was Rama as the noble man and true king that accounts for his becoming such a commanding figure in the rest of South and Southeast Asia, and even in the original homeland of Buddhism, Northern India, and Nepal. Such was the case in Sri Lanka, Cambodia, Java, and Thailand, where Buddhism remained the official state religion but the Rama legend provided the legitimizing myth shown by the Khmer rulers in their monuments at Angkor Wat, as well as by the court rituals and name of Rama adopted by the early rulers of the reigning Thai monarchy. Likewise, even in Islamic countries like Malaya, Indonesia, and among the Moros of the Philippines, the ethos of the Ramayana has survived in the native arts and traditional literature.

Note, however, that this ideal of nobility in the *Ramayana* is grounded in the emerging civility of the Indian tradition in the Classic age. While critical of the conduct of those who represent the established order, the critique is based on classic values, raising them to a still higher level. It remains in touch with the kinship values that persist into a new urbanizing civilization still largely based on an agricultural economy, and on agricultural communities still bound to a kinship ethic. Nobility as an overarching ideal may stand in some tension with family loyalties of this latter type, but together they continue to represent a continuum of civilized values. At this stage, then, the advancing of Rama's nobility does not constitute a radical break with the past, but an attempted revitalization of it—renewal of tradition through criticism of the present.

If the *Ramayana* is an epic celebrating the ideal virtues of the leadership class (that is, its true nobility), in the *Kama Sutra* of Vatsyayana (100 to 500 CE) we find a classic statement of what might be seen as its complement, that is, civility among ordinary householders. Here the lifestyle of the householder comes closest to representing the public life of the average citizen, but it is to be understood in the context of the prevailing caste system, with its differentiation of roles among the *brahmans* (priests), *kshatriya* (warriors), *vaisya* (farmers and merchants) and *shudra* (menials), as well as in terms of the four classic pursuits or aims of life: moral duty *(dharma)*, power and wealth *(artha)*, pleasure *(kama)* and spiritual freedom *(moksha)*.

Among these the pursuit of pleasure by the city dweller and householder is the prime subject of the *Kama Sutra*. This is by no means an exclusive pursuit, or one restricted to the householders of the *vaisya* caste. In the *Kama Sutra* it is made clear that religion, power, profit, and pleasure are complementary, and indeed the pursuit of pleasure is seen as conditional on the satisfaction of these other values— that is, some degree of power or wealth is prerequisite to the pursuit of pleasure, just as, in fact, its pursuit is to be governed to some degree by religious restraint.

As set forth in the *Kama Sutra,* pleasure is a leisured pursuit, a diversion for the well-to-do. The list of such leisure arts is a long one, including singing, dancing, playing musical instruments, writing and drawing, acting, stage performance, ornamentation and cosmetics. It also includes knowledge of many technical arts, language skills, manly arts of the sword, staff, and bow and arrow, cockfighting, gambling, and so forth. As is well known, how to make love is prominent among the arts featured by the *Kama Sutra.*

Although these many skills are recommended for all "citizens" capable of mastering them, they are clearly intended for the man-about-town (whatever his class). They define the cultivated gentleman, and may be thought of as a kind of cultured gentility—something that neither aims at the nobility of a demanding *noblesse oblige* on the one hand, nor, on the other, does it speak to a generalized morality among citizens at large, understood as entailing some sense of civic virtue and responsibility.

A chapter entitled "The Life of a Citizen"[7] details many of the items of personal conduct, bodily care, and cosmetic enhancement that befit the life of a leisured householder, but it also identifies the social activities in which he engages:

1. Going to festivals in honor of the deities
2. Salons (gatherings of both sexes)
3. Drinking parties
4. Picnics
5. Other social diversions.[8]

Significantly, the text identifies the women included in the social gatherings as "public women," namely courtesans, a distinct professional class of women whose company and talents are enjoyed outside the home. Here "public" differentiates this special class from the wives who are confined to home as private possessions of the householder. Although the courtesans as public women are more available to a pleasure-seeking clientele, in a sense they exist for the personal gratification of the male and to this extent they represent a privatization of the public sphere by the well-to-do gentleman whose gentility is that of the connoisseur: a cultivated refinement of the life of the senses, little connected with any sense of public or civic responsibility. In fact this gentility no more qualifies as a generalized civility than does the ethic of the family, or even of the caste organization itself, as a breeding ground for the values that are understood to sustain the social order at large.

The inherent paradox of this concept of the citizen as a man-about-town is that he can expect to command general or public respect by all for his social skills and refined tastes, but, as the text says after reciting the kinds of amusements he indulges in, these are "followed by a person who diverts himself alone in company with a courtesan, as well as by a courtesan who can do the same in company with her servants or with [individual] citizens."[9]

A more likely source for an account of the conduct appropriate to citizens as ordinary civilians is found in a text written for Indian princes and statesmen, the *Sukranitisara* of Shukracharya (10th–16th c.?), which, besides prescribing the duties of the ruling class, also offers general rules for people who are expected to be law-abiding and civil in their conduct toward one another. Indeed, although primarily intended to proffer useful advice to the king, its chapter on "General Rules of Morality" speaks of these rules as "common to the king and commonwealth (people)"[10]

Much of the advice offered is prudential and of a general sort, as for instance: "One should always master the world by love, association, praise, submission, service, artifice, arts, words, wisdom, affection, simplicity, valor, charity, learning, getting up or coming in front to receive superiors, words spoken with cheerful smiles, and benefits rendered"(114 no. 302).

At the same time the advice is practical in the worldly sense, as when the treatise speaks realistically about the importance of wealth. "One should carefully preserve wealth that can maintain life in the future"(116 no. 356). "So long as there is wealth, one is respected by all. But the man without wealth, though well-qualified, is deserted even by wife and sons."(116 no. 362). "In this world wealth is the means to all pursuits, so men should try to acquire it by good ways and means, e.g. by good learning, good service, valor, agriculture, usury, stone-keeping, arts or begging" (116 no. 364). "One should practice whatever means makes a man wealthy" (116 no. 368).

Though high priority is given to the acquiring of wealth, it is, however, by no means a final good in itself. "After having amassed wealth one should maintain his family. The wise man should never pass a day without giving something away" (118, no. 413). "Woe to the man who does not take care to maintain his kith and kin. All his virtues go for nothing" (112, no. 252). "In this world there is nothing more capable of subduing others than charity and simplicity. The moon that has waned through gifts, when waxing, is beautiful in the form of a curve"(119, no. 432).

In general, the *Sukraniti* seeks a mean among competing values. "Excess is ruinous, so one should avoid it." "Poverty comes through excessive charity; insult through excessive cupidity, and foolishness is begotten of excessive zeal"(119, no. 432, 441).

Pervading the text is the need for a sense of balance, with prime emphasis on realism and prudential judgment. "One should carry the enemy on one's shoulders so long as he is more powerful than oneself, but after learning that his strength has been impaired, one should break him down as a vessel against a stone"(120, no. 469).

A charming illustration of a more gentle wisdom is found in "It is better to cover feet with shoes than to try to cover the whole earth with leather. Ignorance is better than vanity due to little learning"(123, no. 574).

One cannot expect to find complete consistency in a collection of aphorisms the trenchancy of which is very much adapted to particular contexts. The general context here assumes the prevalence of a given social order. Much of the practical advice, for instance, has to do with marriage arrangements in a society wherein family and caste status are powerful determinants of one's success in life. Likewise, the performance of duty as defined by caste roles is a general imperative. This being the case, the general rules of morality presented here as "ordinary rules of social polity" are unlikely to encourage political citizenship on the part of anyone other than the upper classes expected to serve the ruler in official functions. Thus it is said that one "should glorify the lord whom one serves and never disparage him; one should always be alert in his service and try always to please him"(118, no. 430, 431). But except for those in such service, "One should not discuss royal policies in an assembly"(115, no. 332).

Inevitably, this restricted scope of political or social activity has its implications for women who, left to themselves, or acting on their own, are seen as a likely source of trouble: "One should not leave his place by making the young wife dependent on herself. Women are the roots of evils. Can young females be left with others?"(126, no. 643). Indeed, the very nature of women is such that one cannot allow them much of a public role, given their proclivities for evil: "The eight natural defects of women are mendacity, rashness, attachment, foolishness, greed, impurity, cruelty and vanity"(115, no. 332).

A classic work of south India, the *Kural* (500–600 CE), attributed to Tiruvalluvar, deals with the same traditional goals of life as the *Sukraniti:* virtue, wealth, and love. Like the *Ramayana,* it assumes that the high ideals set forth for kings are exemplary for all humankind. Thus the king is spoken of in these terms:

The world looks up to heaven for rain
And his subjects to their king for justice.
The king's sceptre provides the base
For scripture and right conduct.
The king who rules cherishing his people
Has the world at his feet.
The king who rules according to the law
Never lacks rain and corn.
Not his spear but a straight sceptre
Is what gives a monarch his triumph."[11]

The high level of conduct called for in the king requires many of the same values as are celebrated in the *Ramayana:* self-restraint, truthfulness, fidelity to one's kin, mildness and gentleness, compassion, fortitude, and so on. But these virtues, while available to all, are presumed to be nourished in the bosom of the family and most likely to be sustained by the sense of honor found in a traditional kin-based ethic:

Integrity and shame are natural
Only to the well-born.
Men of birth will never slip
In conduct, truth and refinement.
A smiling face, a generous heart, sweet words and no scorn
Are said to mark the well-born.(116)

This nobility, though high-born, is marked by gentility and courtesy to all:

Gentle kin and kindliness combined
Constitute courtesy. . . .
The world loves the gentility which combines
Justice with benevolence. . . .

It is base to be discourteous
Even to one's enemies. . . .
Noble men will not accept the world itself
Unfenced by nicety.(120–122)

To this gentility and nicety, moreover, a sense of *noblesse oblige* attaches:

There is nothing more glorious that to persist
In the advance of the community.
Ceaseless zeal and wisdom—these two—
Advance the community. . . .
True manliness is the taking on
Of the leadership of one's people.(167)

The word *kudi* translated here as "community" normally has the connotation of "family" or "clan." Understandably, the modern translator wishes to extend its meaning to a larger community(167, n1021), but this transition to a larger public became the issue faced later by twentieth-century leaders like Gandhi, who sought to enlist the values so warmly nourished in the traditional family for the service of the larger community of the nation-state. For Gandhi this meant resisting the fierce loyalties of a traditional communalism, but precisely therein lay the dilemma of modern reformers trying to extract and adapt ancient values from the institutions that had nurtured them, when the latter were themselves so challenged by the forces of modern life that almost any traditionalism, so embattled, could congeal and harden into blind fundamentalism.

In twentieth-century India, continuity with tradition has been marked by extreme contrasts of civility and incivility, commonality and divisive communalism. On the one hand, there is the Ramayana's ideal of self-restraint and nonviolence as an inspiration for the nonviolent civil disobedience of Mahatma Gandhi, who died with the name of Rama on his lips, the victim of a Hindu assassin. Then, in the same ironical contrast, there is the burning down of a Muslim mosque at Ayodhya by devotees of Rama who saw it as an offense to a site sacred to him, but who thereby set off a wave of savage communal rioting with enormous loss of human life.

Gandhi is famous for his response to the question "what do you think of Western civilization," to which he reportedly replied, "I think it would be a good idea." Actually, if one looks at what he wrote about Western civilization, one wonders whether he even thought that it *could* be a good idea. He was sweeping in his criticism of the West as irreligious and immoral: "This civilization takes note neither of morality nor of religion. Its votaries calmly state that their business is not to teach religion. . . . This civilization is irreligious and it has taken such a hold on the people of Europe that those that are in it are half-mad."[12] "Many problems can be solved by remembering that money is their God. . . . They wish to convert the whole world into a vast market for their goods"(40–41). Moreover, Gandhi is particularly scornful of what many would consider one of the greatest British contributions to civilization: parliamentary rule. "Parliaments are really emblems of slavery"(37). "It is a superstition and ungodly thing to believe that an act of a majority binds a minority . . . that we should obey laws whether good or bad is a new-fangled notion"(80–81).

Gandhi's answer to the corruption and corrosion of modern Western civilization is simple. To the question what is true civilization, he replies: "The answer to that question is not difficult. I believe that the civilization India has evolved is not to be beaten in the world"(60). "The tendency of the Indian civilization is to elevate the moral being, that of Western civilization is to propagate immorality"(63). "The condition of India is unique. It's strength is immeasurable. We need not therefore refer to the history of other countries. I have drawn attention to the fact that, when other civilizations have succumbed, the Indian has survived many a shock"(66).

Granting the hyperbole that must be allowed to any Indian nationalist leader trying to rally his people in resistance to foreign rule, the more important question here is whether true civilization as Gandhi conceives of it would be governed by a civility that linked all humankind. At that point the question is raised whether Western civilization could become "a good idea" by becoming "Indianized" (if not in general, at least so far as their role in India is concerned). To think that an impossibility, says Gandhi, "is equivalent to saying that the English have no humanity in them. . . . To believe that what has not occurred in history will not occur is to argue disbelief in the dignity of man."

Whether that "humanity" and "dignity" could take the form of a cross-civilizational civility is another question. For Gandhi true civilization is based on the village, handicraft economy, and on a simple religiosity grounded in a fundamentalist morality. The forefathers of India "reasoned that large cities were a snare and a useless encumbrance and that people would not be happy in them, that there would be gangs of thieves and robbers, prostitution and vice flourishing in them and that poor men would be robbed by rich men. They were therefore satisfied with small villages"(62).

In the small-village context it was natural for Gandhi to conceive of civilization as "that mode of conduct which points out the path of duty. Performance of duty and obser-vance of morality are convertible terms. To observe moral-ity is to attain mastery over our mind and our passions. So doing, we know ourselves. The Gujarati equivalent for civi-lization means 'good conduct'"(61).

There is significance here in Gandhi's invoking the prime traditional value of the "path of duty," the same as followed by Rama, and in his ready equation of it with his own local, Gujarati understanding of civilization. This re-duction of civilization to a ground-level, fundamentalist morality represent both the bedrock strength of Gandhi's movement and its limitation in coping with the problems of a larger world. Gandhi had great faith in his own soul-force and in passive resistance as the answer to all problems, but his leadership relied on a powerful subjectivity that did not easily lend itself to bridging communal and cultural differ-ences—beliefs as deep and uncompromising as his own.

It is understandable then that the Indian nationalist movement had to compromise on his principles: to agree to the creation of Pakistan (against his wishes), and to accept the need for parliamentary politics and majority rule as a way of bridging communal differences that a fundamental-ist morality alone could not cope with.

Thus for all of the moral virtue which Gandhi nobly sought to inculcate in politics, it has remained a problem how it could contribute to a new civility without developing at the same time some new definition of a broader human-ity and some new practice for a wider community.

3

Buddhist Spirituality and Chinese Civility

At this point we turn back to the "nobility" of the Buddha, and ask whether, as Buddhism spread to the East, it did not encounter similar questions as to how its "nobility of the spirit," its world-transcending pursuit of Nirvana, would relate to the indigenous civilities of East Asia.

China, as we have seen, was mostly Confucian in regard to its civil institutions, at least insofar as they reflected the Confucian concepts clustered around the term *wen* (literate culture, civilization, civil virtues versus military power). We recall that when Confucius distinguished civil governance from government relying on force and coercion, he characterized the former as based on "virtue and the rites," with the "rites" understood as consensual, customary practices giving formal expression to natural, moral sentiments. Among these practices, one of the most common was "bowing"—showing respect to parents, ancestors, elders, the ruler—rituals embodying the hierarchy of Confucian moral and social priorities. In the early history of Chinese Buddhism, however, a leading Chinese monk, Hui-yuan (334–

417), wrote a famous text, "A Monk Does Not Bow Down to a King," in which he asserted the independence of the Buddhist clergy from such customary observances. Monks pursued a higher religious calling and were not subject to civil authority. Buddhist laymen, like other laymen, were obliged by the customary etiquette to acknowledge respect for and loyalty to the sovereign, but the Buddhist clergy, by the nature of their life and lofty religious aims, were far removed from ordinary men. Hui-yuan says:

> If one examines the broad essentials of the teachings of the Buddha, one will see that they distinguish between those who leave the household life and those who remain in it. . . . Those who revere the Buddhist laws but remain in their homes are subjects who are obedient to the transforming powers [of temporal rulers]. Their feelings have not changed from the customary, and their course of conduct conforms to the secular world. Therefore this way of life includes the affection of natural kinship and the proprieties of obedience to authority. Decorum and reverence have their basis herein, and thus they form the basis of the doctrine.[1]

No doubt it was a similar respect for established custom in civilized society that had led Buddhists in India and other South Asian countries to leave the established social and political order intact rather than try to change it or challenge it to reform. But they should abandon it nevertheless for the sake of a religious life that followed its own rules—the traditional religious rules or injunctions known as the *vinaya*, based essentially on the Buddhist ethic of the noble Eightfold Path leading to Nirvana. Thus Hui-yuan argues:

He who has left the household life is a lodger beyond the earthly [secular] world, and his ways are cut off from those of other beings. The doctrine by which he lives enables him to understand that woes and impediments come from having a body, and that by not maintaining the body one terminates woe. . . .

If the determination of woe does not depend on the maintenance of the body, then he does not treasure the benefits that foster life. This is something in which the principle runs counter to physical form and the Way is opposed to common practice. Such men as these commence the fulfillment of their vows with the putting away of ornaments of the head [shaving the head] and realize the achievement of their ideal with the changing of their garb. . . . Since they have changed their way of life, their garb and distinguishing marks cannot conform to the secular pattern.[2]

Thus far in his discourse Hui-yuan speaks for a religious path that closely resembles the *Dhammapada*'s heroic ideal of spiritual nobility, calling on the monk to separate himself from ordinary society and congregate with like-minded aspirants to emancipation from the world. Note especially that Hui-yuan's is not an argument for freedom of religious conscience in general, since no similar claim is made for the spiritual autonomy of the layman. Rather, the claim is for a special immunity to be granted to those who dedicate themselves to the attainment of the higher religious goal. Eventually, as Hui-yuan goes on to say, once the initial break and breakthrough are made, the spiritual benefits of this solitary achievement will accrue charismatically to the secular order and advance the salvation of humanity as a whole.

In this latter projection Hui-yuan presages the more expansive view of universal salvation offered by Mahayana Buddhism, but the main point he makes in the body of the tract is the starting point—the need to be emancipated from the secular world as a condition for achieving spiritual liberation—without which one cannot be of much help to the world.

An alternative to this route, however, and one which becomes much more typical of Chinese Mahayana Buddhism as a whole, is offered by the *Vimalakirti Sutra,* which counterposes the ideal of the religious layman to that of the sequestered monk. In the *Vimalakirti Sutra* the role of the *arhat* (the monk in the *Dhammapada*) is downgraded in comparison to the virtuous layman Vimalakirti, who remains in society and is effectively all things to all men. "Effectively," because he is the embodiment of expedient means—that is, whatever means are most efficacious in accomplishing the salvation of all beings. Here universal salvation is advanced as the explicit aim of the bodhisattva (who for that reason selflessly refrains from leaving the world) in contrast to the *arhat,* who is generally presented in Mahayana scriptures as self-absorbed, proud, stubborn, and indifferent to the salvation of others. In the *Vimalakirti Sutra,* Nirvana is no longer the antithesis of Samsara (the world of ordinary experience). Rather, the two are equated, and the achievement of Buddhahood, as co-implicated with ordinary life and sense experience, thus becomes the salvific embodiment of a wisdom and compassion that are as inseparable as soul and body—the wisdom of emptiness always open to the promptings of compassion, but compassion always qualified by the wisdom (law) of Emptiness.

Here wisdom is the insight that recognizes the insubstantiality of all things, their essential emptiness, while compassion, the impulse to share this wisdom with others still sunk in delusion and suffering, is at the same time also "empty." Thus whatever the diverse means that may be effective in reaching the consciousness (including the sense consciousnesses) of different beings, they are essentially forms of spiritual guidance and uplift—aimed at transforming consciousness rather than changing the social world or activating a moral conscience grounded in human sentiments.

That this new consciousness incorporates but also goes beyond the world of ordinary experience—collapsing the distinction between Nirvana and Samsara, wisdom and illusion—is contained in the view of Non-duality which is, in the end, expressible by Vimalakirti only by silence.

The *Sutra*'s discussion of "Entering the Gate of Non-duality" gives the explanations of this by different bodhisattvas, including the bodhisattva Jewel Crowned King, who says:

The correct way and the erroneous way constitute a duality. But one who dwells in the correct way does not make distinctions, saying, "This is erroneous, This is correct." By removing oneself from both, one may enter the gate of non-duality . . .

When the various bodhisattvas had finished one by one giving their explanations, they asked Manjushri, "How then does the bodhisattva enter the gate of non-duality?"

Manjushri replied, "To my way of thinking, all dharmas are without words, without explanations, without purport, without cognition, removed from all questions and answers. In this way one may enter the gate of non-duality."

Then Manjushri said to Vimalakirti, "Each of us has given an explanation. Now, sir, it is your turn to speak. How does the bodhisattva enter the gate of non-duality?"

At that time Vimalakirti remained silent and did not speak a word.

Manjushri sighed and said, "Excellent, excellent! Not a word, not a syllable—this truly is to enter the gate of non-duality!"[3]

In China the equating of Nirvana and Samsara and the equalizing of all values was given expression in a variety of expedient means, but three of them have particular relevance to our question of how nobility, according to this concept of non-dualist wisdom, would relate to Chinese civility.

The most popular and influential illustrations of expedient means in Mahayana Buddhism are found in the famous *Lotus Sutra*. Here the parables of the Burning House and of the Lost Son show how the father (representing the Buddha) saves his children (deluded beings) by gradually weaning them from their limitations and misconceptions, employing expedient means that appeal to these very limitations, and leading them finally to an awareness of greater possibilities that lie ahead (the realization of Buddhahood). These are parables of spiritual liberation from the travails of ordinary life, leaving them behind, but in a way that expands the scope of salvation beyond that of the monk who relies mostly on his own efforts to achieve the spiritual nobility taught in the *Dhammapada*.

Another story in the *Lotus* further emphasizes the instant availability of these expedient means in the miraculous transformation of the daughter of the Dragon King into a Buddha. The passage is introduced by a question put to one of the Buddha's disciples, Manjushri:

Bodhisattva Wisdom Accumulated questioned Manjushri, saying, "This *sūtra* is very profound, subtle and wonderful, a treasure among *sūtras,* a rarity in the world. Are there perhaps any living beings who, by earnestly and diligently practicing this *sūtra,* have been able to attain Buddhahood quickly?"

Manjushri replied, "There is the daughter of the dragon king Sāgara, who has just turned eight. Her wisdom has keen roots and she is good at understanding the root activities and deeds of living beings. . . . She is fully endowed with blessings, and when it comes to conceiving in mind and expounding by mouth, she is subtle, wonderful, comprehensive, and great. Kind, compassionate, benevolent, yielding, she is gentle and refined in will, capable of attaining *bodhi.*" . . .

At that time Shariputra said to the dragon girl, "You suppose that in this short time you have been able to attain the unsurpassed way. But this is difficult to believe. Why? Because a woman's body is soiled and defiled, not a vessel for the Law. How could you attain the unsurpassed *bodhi*? The road to Buddhahood is long and far-stretching. Only after one has spent immeasurable *kalpas* pursuing austerities, accumulating deeds, practicing all kinds of *pāramitās,* can one finally achieve success. Moreover, a woman is subject to the five obstacles. First, she cannot become a Brahma heavenly king. Second, she cannot become the king Shakra. Third, she cannot become a devil king. Fourth, she cannot become a wheel-turning sage king. Fifth, she cannot become a Buddha. How then could a woman like you be able to attain Buddhahood so quickly?"

At that time the dragon girl had a precious jewel worth as much as the thousand-millionfold world which she presented to the Buddha. The Buddha immediately accepted it. The dragon girl said to Bodhisattva Wisdom Accumulated and to the venerable one, Shariputra, "I presented the precious jewel and the World-Honored One accepted it—was that not quickly done?"

He replied, "Very quickly!"

The girl said, "Employ your supernatural powers and watch me attain Buddhahood. It will be even quicker than that!"

At that time the members of the assembly all saw the dragon girl in the space of an instant change into a man and carry out all the practices of a bodhisattva, immediately proceeding to the spotless World of the south, taking a seat on a jeweled lotus, and attaining impartial and correct enlightenment. With the thirty-two features and the eighty characteristics, he expounded the wonderful Law for all living beings everywhere in the ten directions.[4]

Some recent writers have seen this story as affirming gender equality in Buddhism, but it is an equality of spiritual attainment and not a social equality. It confirms the traditional view in Buddhism of women as inferior to men and, without contradicting it, asserts that the power of the *Lotus* is such that the dragon girl could transcend her inferior social condition to achieve spiritual liberation. In the *Lotus* as a whole the inferior status of women is accepted, and a sex change (as here) or rebirth as a man is a prerequisite to the attainment of Buddhahood as a man. The leading Japanese exponent of the *Lotus*, Saichō (767–822), said of the dragon girl: "She is an animal, (one of the lower levels of the) six destinies [realms], obviously the result of bad karma. She is female and clearly has faculties which are not good. She is young and thus has not been practicing with religious masters for a long time. And yet, the wondrous power of the *Lotus Sutra* endows her with the two adornments of wisdom and merit."[5]

Of this a recent thorough scholar of the subject has further said:

> This interpretation accepts the premise that women generally lack the capacity for full Enlightenment. It is only the miraculous power of the *Lotus Sutra* that makes the dragon girl's spiritual achievements possible, not the lack of impediment imposed by sex or gender.
>
> A gender-transformation narrative that is fully consistent with gender justice would affirm the capacity of both men and women for full Buddhahood. This requires more than those passages in the *Lotus Sutra* that assert the irrelevance of gender but continue to posit a sex change as a prerequisite to Enlightenment.[6]

Indeed, this is an interpretation consistent with the role and message of Vimalakirti as reported above. If his message is a final silence, his role is to bring his enlightening message to all men in a form adapted to their given condition, not to change that condition or the social order. As a bodhisattva of both wisdom and compassion, Vimalakirti is similar to the archetypical bodhisattva Avalokiteshvara (Guanyin, Kannon), often spoken of as the Goddess of Mercy or Compassion. Iconographically, Guanyin is represented as carrying the lamp of enlightenment to all humankind, to dispel the illusions which are the source of suffering. This, however, is not the same as the torch of the Statue of Liberty or the flame of freedom that Julia Ward Howe saw in the Union campfires of her "Battle Hymn of the Republic," fighting to free the slaves. The liberating silence of Vimalakirti is not the Emancipation Proclamation. Another example of this spiritual equalizing, which bypasses social classes, appears in the so-called *Platform Sutra* of the Sixth Patriarch (ca. 780). In a sense the title of the work overrides the dichotomy between Buddhahood and ordinary humanity, for traditionally "sutra" meant authoritative scripture as found in the direct teaching of the Buddha Shakyamuni, but here a later patriarch is accepted as a living Buddha and his words are accepted as having the same status as the authentic teaching of the original Buddha himself. In this case, however, the Sixth Patriarch is a commoner with virtually no social or cultural credentials, who becomes self-enlightened by direct personal intuition. His realization of Buddhahood is essentially not based on any instruction; it is only confirmed and authenticated by his master and predecessor as Patriarch. Thus the expression in later Chan (Zen) Buddhism, that this was a tradition "transmitted [directly] from mind-to-mind outside the [received] doctrine."

Here the equalizing of things takes the form of a social egalitarianism, since Hui-neng (later to become the Sixth Patriarch) is an illiterate commoner, who exemplifies the lowest common denominator of humankind, not only socially but culturally. He has no credentials whatever. This is equal opportunity for native intelligence. Another meaning attaches, however, to his becoming the successor to the Fifth Patriarch and standing in a line of succession the authority for which has no basis in doctrine and bears no public certification. It is an ineluctable succession imparted wordlessly from mind to mind. Wordless, it is subject to no logical or conceptual test; imparted from mind to mind, its outward authority depends on nothing more than the claim to have succeeded to a factual lineage. As a matter of personal religious experience, the question of credentials is of little consequence, except perhaps to the extent that it might affect one's choice of a teacher. But it inevitably attaches to the borderline between lay and clerical: if rulers accepted Hui-yuan's distinction between the two, as some did, they still had to decide whom to recognize as clerical and qualified to enjoy the immunities and exemptions Hui-yuan claimed for the monk. This came to involve the licensing of monks, and eventually the establishment of superintendencies to ascertain whether monks were not simply taking advantage of the immunities, while neglecting, if not actually violating, the disciplinary rules that were supposed to serve in place of secular law.

Thus there was no neat line of demarcation between clerical and lay, and the problem of regulating the conduct of monks proved a chronic difficulty. Here an episode in the Yuan (Mongol dynasty) may illustrate the problem. The Mongols were at least nominally Buddhist (Lamaist) and inclined to be tolerant of religions generally as long as they kept the peace. But, as conquerors of China, the Mongols showed their "civility" by reestablishing the civil service examination system, now and for the first time based on the Neo-Confucian curriculum and Zhu Xi's version of the Four Books. When, therefore, they faced the question of licensing Buddhist monks, it was natural enough for them to want to deal with the problem of credentials on the same basis—an examination of one's knowledge of texts, in this case the Buddhist scriptures. Yet when the proposal was made at court to examine monks on their knowledge of

Buddhist scriptures, a leading Chan (Zen) master went to the Mongol chancellor to protest. Here is the record of the encounter between them:

> The Chancellor said: "I have received a sacred [i.e., Imperial] edict to send officials to take charge of the examinations on the scriptures. Those who are able to read will be allowed to continue as clergy; and those who are illiterate will be ordered to return to the laity."
>
> The Master responded: "I am a rustic monk myself, I never look at scriptures and do not know a single word."
>
> The Chancellor asked: "If you cannot read, how could you become a senior monk?"
>
> The Master rejoined with: "Is the honorable Great Official able to read [the scriptures]?"[7]

Implicit in the Chan master's stated position were two irreducible dilemmas: the inexpressibility of religious truth in words, and the impossibility of stating who had final authority to interpret scripture. Since the government would no doubt face the latter dilemma in finding prospective examiners, not surprisingly it decided to back off. In a face-saving formula that one would think could only come out of comic opera, or perhaps from the wildly whimsical Ming novel, *A Journey to the West,* it was agreed that "the examination would take place, but no candidates would fail."[8]

After all, then, the Chan master proved in this instance to be more equal than others. But it was only the equality of a mutual standoff, a tacit agreement to do nothing. How then could one move beyond a stalemate, bridge the gap between a private experience of enlightenment to a public consensus on political and social action? For those mindful of it in China and Japan, this remained a vexing question.

A partial answer to it is found in the outcome of the sparring that continued after Hui-yuan's time over the unresolved question of the state's authority and control over the Buddhist clergy.

Buddhism's early claim to exist beyond the authority of the state, as asserted by Hui-yuan, was radically transformed in Tang China, when institutionally it became an arm of the state. The institution of "superintendent of the Buddhist clergy (*samgha*)," which first appeared under the Northern Wei in the mid-fifth century, marked the inception of this transformation. The superintendent headed a bureaucracy staffed by lay officials or nominal "monks" charged with oversight of monastic affairs. He was not the head of an autonomous religious organization, but rather an appointee of the Emperor and given tonsure by the Emperor's hand.

The religious rationale for this government-run Buddhism was supplied by the first superintendent, Faguo, who justified monks' service of the government by directly identifying the Emperor as the Buddha. In contrast to Hui-yuan's rigorous defense of clerical independence, Faguo said that "Taizu is enlightened and loves the Way. He is in his very person the Thus-Come One [the Buddha]. Monks must and should pay him all homage. . . . He who propagates the teaching of the Buddha is the lord of men. I am not doing obeisance to the Emperor, I am merely worshiping the Buddha." In response to this acceptance of state authority, the anonymous author of the *Perfect Wisdom Sutra of the Humane King Who Wishes to Protect His State* saw superintendency as a sure sign of the corruption of Buddhism in the last days or decadent End of the Teaching, saying, "If any of my disciples, monks or nuns accept state registration and serve as officials, they are not my disciples."[9]

As an alternative to Buddhism's serving the state, the *Sutra of the Humane King* proposes that the state and Buddhism serve each other. Using the vocabulary of Chinese monarchy, the scripture asserts that "humane" or "benevolent" kings *(renwang)* practice "outer protection" *(waihu)*, a protection that involves the patronage of an independent clergy who practice the "inner protection" *(neihu)* of the bodhisattva virtue of "forbearance" *(ren)*. The pun on the term *ren,* substituting "forbearance" for "humaneness," is the basis of the scripture and the starting point of all of its commentaries. Thus, according to an early seventh-century *Commentary on the Sutra of the Humane King,* the ruler who protects Buddhism thereby protects the state.

Because the humane king *(renwang)* explicates the Teaching and disseminates virtue here below, he is called "humane." Because he has transformed himself, he is called "king." The humane king's ability is to protect *(hu)*. What is protected is the state. This is possible because the humane king uses the Teaching to order the state. Now if we consider the Highest Perfect Wisdom *(Prajñāpāramitā)*, its ability is to protect. The humane king is he who is protected. Because he uses the Highest Perfect Wisdom the humane king is tranquil and hidden. Thus, if he uses his ability to propagate the Teaching, the king is able to protect [the state], and it is the Highest Perfect Wisdom which is the [method of] protection. Moreover, one who is humane is forbearing *(renzhe ren ye)*. Hearing of good he is not overjoyed; hearing of bad he is not angry. Because he is able to hold to forbearance in good and bad, therefore he is called forbearing *(ren)*.[10]

Here the scripture's adroit use of language to reorder the relationship between religion and the state is coupled with Mahayana teachings of Perfect Wisdom (of Non-dualism or Emptiness). Amoghavajra's eighth-century recension of the text further accentuates these teachings through the addition of such passages as the following based on the dialectics of negation and Non-dualism:

At that time the World-honored One said to King Prasenajit, "By what signs do you contemplate the Thus-Come One?" King Prasenajit answered, "I contemplate his body's real signs; [I] contemplate the Buddha thus: without boundaries in front, behind, and in the middle; not residing in the three times and not transcending the three times; not residing in the five aggregates, not transcending the five aggregates; not abiding in the four great elements and not transcending the four great elements; not abiding in the six abodes of sensation and not transcending the six abodes of sensation; not residing in the three realms and not transcending the three realms; residing in no direction, transcending no direction; [neither] illumination [nor] ignorance, and so on. Not one, not different; not this, not that; not pure, not foul; not existent nor non-existent; without signs of self or signs of another; without name, without signs; without strength, without weakness; without demonstration, without exposition; not magnanimous, not stingy; not prohibited, not transgressed; not forbearing, not hateful; not forward, not remiss; not fixed, not in disarray; not wise, not stupid; not coming, not going; not entering, not leaving; not a field of blessings, not a field of misfortune;

without sign, without the lack of sign; not gathering, not dispersing; not great, not small; not seen, not heard; not perceived, not known. The mind, activities, and senses are extinguished, and the path of speech is cut off. It is identical with the edge of reality and equal to the [real] nature of things. I use these signs to contemplate the Thus-Come One."[11]

In this passage the "unboundedness" of the Buddha's body and the principle of universal emptiness in the *Prajñāpāramitā* (expressed in the negation of all determinate views) could also be understood in the more affirmative terms of the Huayan (Avatamsaka) philosophy, namely, the universal tolerance and mutual nonobstruction of all things (expressed as "nothing precludes or bars anything else," *shishi wu ai*, or, politically, anything goes if it serves the higher purposes of Buddhism). Both formulations underlay the practice of Amoghavajra's Esoteric Buddhism or Mystical Teaching, which was predicated on a view similar to Huayan's "True Emptiness [allows for] Mysterious or Wondrous Manifestations *(zhen kong miaoyou)*." Thus mystic rites and incantations could play a part in Esoteric Buddhism's consecration and legitimation of imperial rule, similar to Buddhism's providing a mystique for rulership in South Asia Buddhism.

In Tang China this was notably illustrated by the career of the leading exponent of the Huayan Buddhist philosophy, Fazang (643–712), also a key figure in its transmission to Korea and Japan. Fazang was closely involved in the major political developments of the late seventh-century Tang dynasty—a religious accessory to the rise and fall of the usurping Empress Wu Zitian—but his role was that of an astute politician, opportunistically promoting and exploiting the Empress for his own personal and religious purposes, not that of a significant contributor to any public philosophy, policy, or program.[12]

By the time of Amoghavajra's new recension of the *Sutra of the Humane King,* Chinese Buddhism was unquestionably an arm of the state. His recension deepened its theological component while softening and transforming objections to the monks' service of the government—a transformation motivated by Amoghavajra's role as *saṃgha* superintendent and by his Esoteric Buddhist ideology. Thus, he added a long incantation (*dhāraṇī*) to the text and produced three new commentaries that outlined esoteric rites for invoking the wrathful Kings of Illumination (*ming-wang,* Sanskrit *vidyārāja*) for the defense of the state.

Here the view of the Humane King presented by Amoghavajra, while consistent with the Mahayana Buddhist conception of perfect Wisdom and Vimalakirti's Nondualism, contrasts markedly with the Confucian conception of the human mind-and-heart memorably set forth by Mencius.

All human beings have a mind that cannot bear to see the sufferings of others. The ancient kings had a commiserating mind and accordingly a commiserating government. . . . Here is why I say that all human beings have a mind that commiserates with others. Now, if anyone were suddenly to see a child about to fall in a well, his mind would always be filled with alarm, distress, pity, and compassion. That he would react accordingly is not because he would use the opportunity to ingratiate himself with the child's parents, nor because he would seek commendation from neighbors and friends, nor because he would hate the adverse reputation. From this it may be seen that one who lacks a mind that feels pity and compassion would not be human; one who lacks a mind that feels shame and aversion would not be human; one who lacks a mind that feels modesty and compliance would not be human; and one who lacks a mind that knows right and wrong would not be human. (Mencius 2A:6)

Mencius' point is that the humane king, like all other humans, has "a heart that cannot endure [the suffering of others] (bu ren ren zhi xin)," that naturally commiserates with the sufferings of others or the injustices done to them and feels impelled to remedy these. He is moved by natural moral sentiments of good and evil, right and wrong. Thus Mencius says, "One who lacks a mind that knows right and wrong would not be human." Hence, from the Mencian and, generally the Confucian point of view, a king who forbore from acting on his knowledge of right and wrong could never be called "humane." No humane king could be as "forbearing," tolerant, or noncommittal as Amoghavajra recommends on the basis of his Non-dualist wisdom.

Mencius' view reflects his understanding of human nature and the natural moral sentiments of the human mind-and-heart; Amoghavajra, by contrast, is speaking of the Buddha-nature and asking the king to preserve a Buddha-mind that tolerates anything and everything that may be subsumed under or conduce to Perfect Enlightenment. The incompatibility of the two, as perceived by Confucians early and late, gave rise to continuing debate in China and Korea.

In Japan similar issues arose in a somewhat different setting—a country that entered the civilizational stage with the simultaneous introduction of Buddhism and Confucianism, but that already possessed a preliterate culture strong enough, and deeply embedded enough in the native soil, to affect the terms of the debate over nobility and civility—and thus the historical outcome in politics and culture.

4

Shōtoku's Constitution and the Civil Order in Early Japan

The key figure in the literal defining, if not the actual shaping, of the civilizational issues in early Japan of the sixth and seventh centuries is generally considered to be Prince Shōtoku (573–621), acting as Regent on behalf of Empress Suiko (592–628). Shōtoku was both a devout student of Buddhism as brought to Japan by Korean missionaries in the late sixth or early seventh century, and a statesman who promulgated a charter of civil government known as the Seventeen Article Constitution. This is an extraordinary combination of religious and political concerns and an altogether remarkable document. Though lacking many features of a modern constitution, as a statement of basic principles of governance, his Seventeen Articles are unprecedented for their time and unique in East Asian history.

In China, what served as basic law for imperial dynasties were the exemplary acts of the founding fathers, regarded as setting a model for their dynastic successors, who were obliged to follow them out of filial piety. In this respect family values persisted, with the Emperor claiming to be the paterfamilias of all.

Though Chinese dynasties claimed to rule over a universal state—one transcending the local claims of tribe and clan—and to that extent aimed at the establishment of a new civil or public order, the dynastic system itself remained a vestige of the kinship system, and as we saw in Rama's India, this entailed a survival of and continuum with many of the traditional values of kin and clan.

This ideal is exemplified in the opening lines of the Confucian *Book of Historical Documents (Shujing;* see *SCT* I), where the sage-king Yao, the ideal ruler and the progenitor of civilized society, is described as one who eschews all force and coercion and governs through the charismatic influence of his benign, fatherly character, radiating out to all of the human family. Thus civilization and the civility proclaimed by the Confucians were marked by the kind of intimate consensual harmony that should prevail in the family. Theoretically, the Chinese dynastic state claimed to live by this ideal, to be perpetuated by the successors to the sage-kings and virtuous founding emperors.

In Shōtoku's Japan too the kinship system prevailed, and powerfully so, amidst the contentions of the great clans that surrounded the court. To overcome this intense domestic strife Shōtoku sought to create a unified state, largely on the models of the great Tang dynasty and the Shilla kingdom, then attempting to unify Korea. To this end, he hoped to construct a meritocratic bureaucracy into which the existing clan leadership could be fitted.

Since Shōtoku's constitution is couched in aphoristic language with a vague Confucian ring to it, the prince appears to turn primarily to China and Confucianism for his general political orientation. Though much involved with Buddhism, he does not look to it for political guidance and makes only one direct reference to it. On the Confucian side, however, we note in the first of his articles an emphasis on conciliation and harmony of the broadest kind—not so clearly tied to "family values" as the paradigm of the sage-king Yao is in the Confucian canon. Shōtoku's Article One reads:

> Harmony is to be valued and contentiousness avoided. All men are inclined to partisanship and few are truly discerning. Hence there are some who disobey their lords and fathers or who maintain feuds with the neighboring villages. But when those above are harmonious and those below are conciliatory and there is concord in the discussion of all matters, the disposition of affairs comes about naturally. Then what is there that cannot be accomplished?[1]

Shōtoku is concerned with dispelling partisanship in general, and recommends "concord in discussion" as a way to deal with it. This is not just a benevolent paternalism, relying simply on the personal virtue and charisma of the sage-king and father of all. As will become clearer in following articles, Shōtoku is projecting a vision of a universal state that promotes the good of all—in other words, a civil order that upholds the public good.

In the second article, Shōtoku refers to Buddhism as a universal religion that can motivate people to overcome their evil propensities. Without his saying so explicitly, one can understand this universal religion as serving the purposes of the universal state by helping to overcome the selfishness and partisanship that produce contention and conflict. In Shōtoku's situation this would apply particularly to local loyalties and clan ties that should now yield to the universal values he is proclaiming. Local allegiances would be dissolved in Buddhist Emptiness—the relativizing of all determinate values in the Non-dualist teaching of Mahayana Buddhism.

Successive articles project a structure of overall imperial authority buttressed by the practice of ritual restraint and decorum on the part of all, and, on the part of those in authority, the practice of fairness and impartiality in the settlement of disputes. All this rests in turn on the engendering of trust and trustworthiness through officials' conscientious attention to public service on behalf of what is right, fair, and impartial.

Yet at times Shōtoku voices doubts that are somewhat out of character for a Confucian. Article 10 says:

> Let us cease from wrath, and refrain from angry looks. Nor let us be resentful when others differ from us. For all men have hearts, and each heart has its own leanings. Their right is our wrong, and our right is their wrong. We are not unquestionably sages, nor are they unquestionably fools. Both of us are simply ordinary men. How can any one lay down a rule by which to distinguish right from wrong? For we are all, one with another, wise and foolish, like a ring which has no end. Therefore, although others give way to anger, let us on the contrary dread our own faults, and though we alone may be in the right, let us follow the multitude and act like them. (52)

Although Shōtoku's skepticism is not wholly out of keeping with Confucius' own example of modesty and caution in asserting the truth, as seen in the *Analects,* and the tone of the *Analects* itself is far from doctrinaire or dogmatic, one is unlikely to find in the Confucian classics anything quite like "How can one lay down a rule by which to distinguish right from wrong?" This certainly does not sound like Mencius, in what we have seen above, when he insisted that the ruler, like all of humankind, can and must recognize right and wrong and act on it, lest he be adjudged "inhumane."

The remaining articles of the constitution display a continuing contrast and tension between Shōtoku's insistence on the supremacy of imperial authority and the difficulty of fixing the truth as the ground of this authority. Thus, on the one hand, he says,"The sovereign is the master of the people of the whole country." And to his officials "who have charge of public affairs" he says, "let it be your task to make clear rewards and punishments" (Art. 12). Above all, the ruler and his minister are duty-bound to uphold the public interest against their own or others' private interest.

> To turn away from that which is private, and to set our faces towards that which is public—this is the path of a minister. Now if a man is influenced by private motives, he will assuredly fail to act harmoniously with others. If he fails to act harmoniously with others, he will assuredly sacrifice the public interest to his private feelings. When resentment arises, it interferes with order, and is subversive of law. Therefore in the first clause it was said that superiors and inferiors should agree together. The purport is the same as this." (Art. 15; 53)

In contrast to this strong assertion of the duty to act for the public interest, are other statements that greatly qualify the picture. While Shōtoku affirms the Confucian view that proper governance rests, not so much on the law, as with the one who administers it, he acknowledges difficulty in finding "the man," meaning the right man for the task.

> When wise men are entrusted with office, the sound of praise arises. If unprincipled men hold office, disasters and tumults multiply. In this world few are born with knowledge; wisdom is the product of earnest reflection. In all things, whether great or small, find the [right] man, and they will surely be well managed; on all occasions, be they urgent or the reverse, meet but with a wise and worthy person, and they will of themselves be amenable. (Art. 7; 52)

By "the man" Shōtoku means a wise and worthy person, what the Confucians would call a sage-king or noble person. Yet here he acknowledges the difficulty of finding a wise man to govern, when he says: "It is not until after a lapse of five hundred years that we at last meet with a wise man, and even in a thousand years we hardly welcome one sage. But if we do not find wise men and sages, wherewithal shall the country be governed?" (Art. 14; 53).

Thus Shōtoku affirms the central importance in government of the wise and worthy person—what Confucians would call the Noble Person—and upholds true nobility according to the Confucian ideal; he then proceeds to qualify the more idealistic and optimistic expectation of the Confucians by citing the rarity of sage-kings and wise ministers. This leaves him with an unresolved conflict, a dilemma he seeks to resolve in the final article, which echoes the need cited in the first article for "conciliation" and "concord" in the discussion of all matters:

> Matters should not be decided by one person alone. They should be discussed with the multitude. In small matters, of less consequence, many others need not be consulted. It

is only in considering weighty matters, where there is a suspicion that they might miscarry, that the multitudes should be involved in debate and discussion so as to arrive at a reasonable conclusion. (Art. 17; 54)

In the West skepticism about placing too great a faith in or reliance upon the ruler alone contributed to the rise of constitutionalism and due process as a way of insuring against the abuse of power or the failure to exercise it properly. Shōtoku's constitution seems to reflect a similar concern. And just as Western constitutions featured some kind of deliberative body and process, something of the sort, though not precisely spelled out, is indicated. The word translated above as literally "multitudes" was probably understood as "the many," or "many others," which left much flexibility as to the participants in the process and how it would work.

In documents of the same era purporting to speak for native tradition we find, as in the *Kojiki*'s (712 CE) account of Japan's origins, distinctly pluralistic conceptions of creation, a celebration of particularistic values, and a picture of irrepressible playfulness among the gods. Along with this there is a disposition to reconcile unruly opposing forces through the consultative process—as, for instance, when the Sun Goddess, insulted by her brother, precipitates a crisis by hiding her light in a cave, and the "myriad deities" *(yao yorozu no kami)* consult together about how to get her to come out. A similar idea is found at the ancient shrine of Izumo, said to embody the spirit of combining opposing elements *(musubi)*; there the deities from the different provinces were believed to hold a congress in the tenth month of the year, each housed in its own little shrine as if in a conference circle around the main shrine (claimed by local priests as an early example of Shinto democracy!). Compare these goings-on with the opening passage of the Confucian *Book of Documents,* where the founding myth is of the sage-king Yao standing alone and fixed, as a perfect personification of wisdom, dignity, and self-restraint, and one can imagine why the Japanese, not entirely comfortable with adopting such a rational, moral ideal as the basis of government rather than hereditary right, would have considered it preferable to just talk things out.

Long after the institutional arrangements projected by Shōtoku and his successors had lapsed, the process of consultation and consensus formation continued in the clan, family, privy, and party councils that have played a key role, often behind the scenes, in Japanese affairs down through the ages. Whether or not these are labeled "democratic" is less important than that this so-called constitution proved to express the spirit or "feel" of the Japanese political process better than any of the legal institutions to which it might have been tied.

The Seventeen Articles are themselves a unique and distinctive product of that process, in dialogue with Asian continental philosophies. Each of the latter had its own part to play. It was this native instinct, celebrated in ancient myth, that Shōtoku evoked and invoked as a natural response to this key issue of public versus private, seeking to give some formal definition to the process of governance while allowing for flexibility in the interpretation of his general principles and their adaptation to the current state of affairs.

Of the three main thrusts of Shōtoku's constitution—the establishment of a civil order presided over by the worthy and wise (a kind of Confucian nobility); the promotion of Buddhism; and the open-ended, pragmatic view of right and wrong, determined by consensual processes—it is safe to say that how the consensus worked would have much to do with how the imported teachings came out in the contention with deeply rooted indigenous forces. Nothing in what Shōtoku says about consultation assumes that it will operate on a level playing field. According to the mythic ideal embodied in the Izumo cult, the gods from all over met together on the basis of equality, symbolically in a row of same-sized shrines, all on the same level. But practically speaking, Japanese society was strongly hierarchical; status and power were factored into any consultation, and consensus implicitly respected this. Great clans and families would have their say.

With regard to the civil order, state building in the early centuries after Shōtoku did show progress, especially in the Taika reforms of 645. In the eighth century a permanent capital was established in Nara as a center of bureaucratic control; and further attempts at strengthening state control were made in the early Heian period. All of these developments were strongly qualified by clan-dominated politics, and the tendency for civil (public) functions to become hereditary (private) functions, according to the traditional mode of Japanese society. A telling example of this is the attempt to establish a Confucian college at Nara to provide instruction that would prepare candidates for a civil service system based on the Chinese Tang dynasty model. Since clan politics and hereditary privilege, not exam-based meritocratic qualifications, increasingly determined the outcome of actual appointment to office, the Confucian college became a dead-letter, with Confucian instruction lodged almost in perpetuity in the Kiyohara family as the vested authority in matters of Confucian learning.

Meanwhile other state projects had a significant part in

defining legal codes and the classical Japanese legacy in history and literature, as well as in the attempted bureaucratization of Shinto, which coexisted with Buddhism. Although the outcome of all these efforts was not in the end the assertion of strong central control, they did establish a nominal formal standard for Japan to be conceived as a unified nation under a single ruler who reigned under the sacred canopy of Heaven and the Sun Goddess. In the long run perhaps the most significant effect of Shōtoku's attempt to assert the primacy of the public good, even if it proved abortive in actual practice, was to establish a theoretical concept of universality and the common good (generally associated with Heaven and "all-under-Heaven") which became the standard of claimed legitimacy for any who sought to exercise authority (that is, those who tried to justify their exercise of power, won by whatever means). Given the prevailing Buddhist sense of uncertainty in regard to right and wrong, and Shōtoku's own pragmatic approach, there were few defined moral constraints on the arrogation and use of power. Once it was seized, however—by whomever—the holder felt an obligation to justify it by invoking a higher, sacred authority or by appealing to some standard of the public welfare (kō or kū) on behalf of all-under-Heaven (tenka).

The second element favored by Shōtoku, Buddhism, had relatively little connection with his primary advocacy of the public sphere, but still played a political role by virtue of its symbiotic ideological association with the ruler. This came to be expressed in terms of "Buddhism Protective of the State," a concept spreading to Japan from Tang China and Shilla (Korea). As an important religious adjunct to the state-building process in all three countries, its rationale, as well as much of its practice, accorded with the doctrines already outlined above in connection with the *Sutra of the Humane King.* Essentially the same rationale was offered by the *Golden Light Sutra,* another text widely promoted by the state in the seventh and eighth centuries.

In short these scriptures assured the ruler that if he would support Buddhism, the Buddhist clergy would support him, and he would enjoy the beneficent religious influences of Buddhism. This was essentially a symbiotic relationship between two separate and distinct organisms. The state (in fact the ruler as personal patron) would protect Buddhism and Buddhism the state, each in its own way.

Though, as in China, the Emperor was almost deified as a Buddha incarnate, he did not usually act as the final authority in doctrinal matters, but only as referee to settle disputes among different sects. Whether or not an actual state system existed, from the time of Buddhism's introduction to Japan the ruler was what counted in this dynastic regime, and the ruler's favor or patronage was the thing at issue, not any Buddhist political program affecting the conduct of state. Then again, as in China, the state (ruler) came to serve as the monitor of religious discipline in temples, monasteries, and nunneries, and the establishment of superintendencies over Buddhist sects in Japan (as in China) made the latter subject to the prevailing pattern in court politics. There, as we shall see, the Fujiwara clan, dominant at court, took on a major role in the administration of the Tendai sect and its headquarters in Mount Hiei, adjacent to and adjunct to the Kyoto court. Since this role became reserved hereditarily to a branch of the Fujiwara, it represented the privatization of religious authority, as distinct from its bureaucratization in China. Thus did Buddhism become fitted into indigenous hierarchical forms—just one of the ways in which it adapted to the Japanese social and cultural scene.

Another measure of this change is what became of Confucian influences—especially the nobility and civility embodied in the Confucian "noble person." As late as the ninth century the idea persisted that study of the Confucian classics was an important adjunct to the preparation even of Buddhist monks, because these texts dealt with secular matters not treated in the Buddhist texts. Vestiges of this idea were found in two leading figures of Heian Buddhism, Saichō (767–822) and Kūkai (774–835).

Saichō, the founder of the great Tendai Buddhist establishment on Mount Hiei, having historically close associations with the Kyoto court, set up a curriculum for his monks that augmented studies of Buddhist scripture, ritual, and meditation techniques with the reading of Confucian texts. He was a strong proponent of the monks' preparing themselves for broad service to human society in fulfillment of the vow of the bodhisattva to help all sentient beings to salvation. Minimizing the traditional Buddhist discipline of the *vinaya,* and reducing substantially the number of traditional precepts or injunctions his monks were obliged to observe, he included among the aims of his program "service to the state (or country) *(kokuyō)."* To this end, Saichō incorporated the vocation of the Confucian "noble person" within his concept of the compassionate bodhisattva: "Buddhists who possess the religious nature are called in the west bodhisattvas; in the east they are known as noble men *(junzi).* They hold themselves responsible for all bad things while they credit others with all good things. Forgetful of themselves, they benefit others. This represents the summit of compassion" (*SJT* I, 146).

Among his specifications for the monks' training program, he required that "During the first six years, the study of the *sūtras* under a master will be their major occupation, with meditation and the observance of discipline their secondary pursuits. Two-thirds of their time will be devoted to Buddhism and the remaining third to the Chinese classics" (148). "If these provisions are followed, men possessing the religious nature will spring up one after another throughout the country, and the Way of the Noble Man shall never die" (147).

When Saichō established his Tendai temple overlooking the Heian capital, he thought of it as a spiritual bastion standing in defense of the state *(Chingo kokka)*, an extension into his own time of the concept of "Buddhism as Protector of the State." His conscious inclusion of Confucian studies, however, and his concept of the Noble Person as necessary to the fulfillment of the boddhisattva's salvific mission reveal his awareness that, without this addition, something would be lacking in the preparation of his monks for service to the state and the public welfare. Of the prime Mahayana scriptures—the *Lotus,* the *Vimalakirti,* the *Sutra of the Humane King,* and *Golden Light Sutra,* among the exoteric texts, and the *Vairochana* among the esoteric texts, none dealt with this. Saichō was unwilling to have his monks (confined though they were on Mount Hiei for twelve years) isolate themselves as a class separate from the rest of society (Hui-yuan's position), but in his curricular choices he recognized the distinct difference between the two traditions and affirmed their complementarity at one and the same time. Yet for all this, Confucian studies did not thrive on Mount Hiei; these were left pretty much to the Kiyowara family.

The second instructive case is that of Kūkai, the leader

of Shingon esotericism. Kūkai was converted to the latter, when, disillusioned with his prospects for an official career, he gave up on his studies at the Confucian College in Nara. Much later in life, having established Mount Kōya as a center of Shingon monasticism and gained a prominent place for esoteric rituals at court, he was caught up in the idea of schooling open to all on the model of public schools in China. It had been a long cherished hope of his, he says, to build a kind of ecumenical center where Confucianism and Daoism would be studied along with Buddhism. A man of remarkably diverse interests and talents himself, he aimed at a comprehensive program of study in an Academy of Arts and Sciences *(Shūgei shūchi-in)*:

> Unless one resorts to these studies, one cannot gain the essentials of how to establish oneself in the world, cannot learn the principles of governing the country, and cannot attain Nirvana on the other shore, terminating the transmigratory life on this shore.
>
> Emperors have built state temples; their subjects have constructed private temples; in this way they have made efforts to spread the Way [Buddhism]. But those who wear robes in the temples study Buddhist scriptures; while scholars and students at the government college study non-Buddhist texts. Thus they are all stuck when it comes to books representing the Three Teachings, and invite capable persons to join. With the aid of these teachings, which can be compared to the sun [Buddhism], the moon [Daoism], and the stars [Confucianism], my sincere desire is to enlighten those who are wandering in the dark down the wrong path, and lead them to the garden of enlightenment mounted on the Five Vehicles. . . .
>
> It may be objected, however: "The government maintains

a state college where the arts and sciences are encouraged and taught. What good is a mosquito's cry [a private school] compared to rumbling thunder [a government school]?"

My reply is: "In the capital of China, a school is set up in each ward to teach the young boys. In each prefecture a school is maintained in order widely to educate promising young students. Because of this, the capital is filled with talented young men and the nation is crowded with masters of the arts. In the capital of our country, however, there is only one government college and no local schools. As a result, sons of the poor have no opportunity to seek knowledge. Those who like to study, but live a great distance from the college, encounter great difficulty traveling to and fro. Would it not be good, then, to establish this school to assist the uneducated?"[2]

Clearly, Kūkai had no intention of equating the Three Teachings. He believed deeply in the superiority of Buddhism and especially its esoteric school, while relegating Confucianism to third place after Daoism, since Confucianism dealt merely with the practical order, not the sublime mysteries of higher religion. Still, one should strive for universality, and if Buddhist teachers are to concentrate on lofty spiritual matters, there should be secular doctors available to teach what Buddhists themselves did not. In this respect, though Kūkai does not go so far as Saichō in his determination that the Confucian "Way of the Noble Person should not perish from the earth," he acknowledged that Confucianism had its own distinctive role to play in fulfillment of Confucius' belief that "All Men are Brothers."[3]

The outcome of Kūkai's effort, however, was no more promising than Saichō's. The academy he set up did not last more than a few years, and the established order persisted, with Buddhist spirituality, Esoteric and Shinto rituals, and Japanese aesthetic culture accommodating to one another, but with Confucianism hardly to be seen in public

For Kūkai's academy, however, this outcome could have been predicted from his own larger vision of the role to be played by Esoteric Buddhism at the Heian Court. Much as Kūkai recognized the political and social relevance of the Confucian classics, Confucianism for him represented only a lower order of reality to be subsumed under the higher order of the Buddhist universal ruler, *chakravartin,* who would wield the sacred power of the mantra and esoteric rituals to exorcize all forms of evil and misfortune.[4]

Institutionally speaking, the Confucian College in Nara was only one part of the legal and administrative system modeled on the Tang, the so-called *ritsu-ryō* system, itself a considerable adaptation of Confucianism to the Chinese dynastic system. Kūkai's advocacy of esoteric Buddhism, in its manifold ritual and aesthetic forms, was meant to endow the Japanese emperor with a religious charisma far more powerful than anything Kūkai recognized in the Tang *ritsu-ryō* system, much less any conception of Confucian rulership already watered down from the teachings of Confucius and Mencius. Hence he could easily identify with the perfect wisdom of the Buddhist *chakravartin,* the wisdom of emptiness, as the ground for the mysticization and ritualization of the Japanese imperial institution.[5] Thus too he could accept the notion of the virtuous king as portrayed in the *Sutra of the Humane King,* that is, with virtue understood not as Confucian humaneness or Mencius' moral conscience but as a universal tolerance that transcends all dualities of true or false, right or wrong, humane or inhumane. In the process Kūkai also naturalized Buddhism in Japanese terms, opening the way to the further aestheticization of court culture, elevating it to the elegant level of Heian period refinement, a high-class gentility well beyond the mundane moral and social engagements that marked the heroic ideal of the Confucian Noble Man.

5

Chrysanthemum and Sword Revisited

To say that Confucianism was little to be seen in public does not mean that it disappeared altogether from Japanese official life in the Heian era (794–1185). Confucian texts remained a formal part of the Chinese studies that educated Japanese were expected to be conversant with, and they were included in the program of the Court Academy (*Daigakuryō*), though not as a necessary or essential qualification for a meritocratic officialdom, but as a cultured adornment of the court aristocracy, probably less important for the Heian gentleman than was the ability to compose good Chinese poetry.

On this score one cannot say that the cultural tone of Heian Japan was all that different from ninth-century Tang China before Han Yü (768–824) made a public issue of the Buddhist rituals being performed at the Chinese court. Confucianism as a public philosophy was at a low ebb in both countries, and the rituals celebrated in either capital, Changan or Kyoto, reflected the dominance in that period of Esoteric Buddhism.

Kūkai had studied in China and on his return to Japan submitted a report entitled "Memorial on the Presentation [to the Emperor] of the list of Newly Imported Sutras." Notwithstanding its reference to Buddhist scripture in the title, the real point of Kūkai's Presentation was less to promote the importance of the doctrinal texts he had brought back than to question the ultimate value of any verbal or written discourse as a means of communicating Buddhist truth. It does, he says, have a proximate use, but nothing to compare with art.

> The law *(dharma)* has no speech, but without speech it cannot be expressed. Eternal truth *(tathatā)* transcends form, but only by means of form can it be understood. Mistakes will be made in the effort to point at the truth, for there is no clearly defined method of teaching, but even when art does not excite admiration by its unusual quality, it is a treasure which protects the country and benefits the people.
>
> In truth, the esoteric doctrines are so profound as to defy their enunciation in writing. With the help of painting, however, their obscurities may be understood. The various attitudes and *mudrās* of the holy images all have their source in Buddha's love, and one may attain Buddhahood at the sight of them. Thus the secrets of the sūtras and commentaries can be depicted in art, and the essential truths of the esoteric teaching are all set forth therein. Neither teachers nor students can dispense with it. Art is what reveals to us the state of perfection. (*SJT* I, 155)

There was nothing new in the idea that the full truth eluded expression in words, as the *Vimalakirti Sutra* had made dramatically clear. But the distinction of esoteric (mysterious, secret) practice from exoteric (explicit, discursive) teaching was an important one; it underscored the resignation of Mahayana Buddhism from the realm of public discourse and open, rational debate, in favor of a variety of expedient or convenient means, many of them more appealing to the senses and even to the passions, as in the saying "the passions in themselves are enlightening." In the Japanese context, "expedient means" meant appealing more to an indigenous religiosity already strongly oriented toward nature and aesthetic experience, as in Shinto.

The further significance of this shift in approach may be seen in the dominance it quickly achieved in major centers of Buddhism, at court, and in the country at large. Even in Saichō's center for the study of the *Lotus Sutra* at Mount Hiei, esotericism soon became dominant. Initially Saichō had thought of establishing a center for scripture study and ecumenical discussion of Buddhist doctrine. But even he recognized the growing importance of esoteric ritual, and his eclectic instincts led him at one point to ask Kūkai humbly for instruction and initiation into a particular rite that the latter had mastered—a request Kūkai ungenerously declined to honor. Nevertheless the successors of Saichō on Mount Hiei saw to it that this Tendai center became fully equipped with esoteric rituals.

Sometimes "esoteric," taken to mean "secret," has been understood as privileging a religious or cultural elite who jealously guarded their vested power over the administration of religion or their own secret knowledge in the practice of rituals. Though such factors cannot be discounted altogether in a very hierarchical aristocratic society, Esoteric Buddhism remained true to the universalistic principles of Mahayana Buddhism, and especially to the unlimited availability of the diverse expedient means adapted to

all levels of society. Popular practice exhibited a wide repertoire of mystical and magical formulae by which Buddhist
rituals would be mediated to any level of society, and indeed it was precisely out of this capacious bag of religious
devices, especially oral incantations, that much of popular
religious practice grew in the medieval period.

What conferred an elite aura and tone on Heian Buddhism was the highly aristocratic and hierarchical nature
of the court itself, the great store it put in both ritual and
art, and its strong, discriminating sense of good taste and
quality. An early indication of this, well before the rise of
Esoteric Buddhism, is given in the classic anthology of Japanese poetry, the *Manyōshū*. As a court-sponsored compilation of Japanese poetry (complementing another anthology
of Chinese poetry by Japanese), the anthology, not surprisingly, included many poems by emperors and their courtiers. It is somewhat surprising, however, to read of an episode at the court of Emperor Tenchi (or Tenji), involving
his prime minister, Fujiwara Kamatari. Together they were
responsible for some of the major state-building efforts in
the mid-seventh century, as Japan tried to catch up with
the advanced civilization of China. Allowing for the relativ-
ity of the term "modern," one can see these two leaders as
performing a historic role comparable, say, to Kaiser Wil-
helm and Otto von Bismarck in the creation of modern
Germany. But in the *Manyōshū* "Collection of Ten Thousand Leaves" (8th c. CE) they appear in quite a different
guise, not as great decision makers in matters of state, but
as arbiters of taste. The text reads:

When the Emperor Tenchi commanded Fujiwara Kamatari, Prime Minister, to judge between the luxuriance of the

blossoms on the spring hills and the glory of the tinted leaves on the autumn hills, Princess Nukada decided the question with this poem.

> *When, loosened from the winter's bonds,*
> *The spring appears,*
> *The birds that were silent*
> *Come out and sing,*
> *The flowers that were prisoned*
> *Come out and bloom;*
> *But the hills are so rank with trees*
> *We cannot see the flowers,*
> *And the flowers are so tangled with weeds*
> *We cannot take them in our hands.*
>
> *But when on the autumn hill-side*
> *We see the foliage,*
> *We prize the yellow leaves,*
> *Taking them in our hands,*
> *We sigh over the green ones,*
> *Leaving them on the branches;*
> *And that is my only regret—*
> *For me, the autumn hills!*[1]

Can one imagine state decision-making taking such form at any other imperial court in the world?

In this anthology, which consciously represents Japanese literary tradition, we can see how thoroughly involved in aesthetic matters the Japanese court was, from very long standing. Much of the poetry concerns passionate love and longing, and the nobility does not appear to be standing above or aloof from this realm of feeling; rather, they are as deeply and openly involved as anyone. Hence, when in the Heian period we meet with a court exhibiting similar heavy involvements, we can appreciate that the aesthetic and emotional side of the native cultural tradition is asserting itself as a strong element of continuity in the life of the elite, and as a powerful influence on the adaptive means to which Buddhism resorted. And if to this one adds the pervasive element of mystery enshrouding Shinto worship and rituals, the coalescence of the two in Japan's assimilation of Esoteric Buddhism is the most natural thing in the world.

The *Tale of Genji,* the monumental novel by Lady Murasaki Shikibu (978?–1015), and the fragmentary observations of Sei Shonagon (967?–?) in her *Pillow Book* are no doubt without peer as works representative of Heian society and culture. And if one is looking for what might be thought of as true nobility in that society, Prince Genji, the "Shining Prince," immediately comes to mind; he is the ideal courtier, the embodiment of all the social and cultural graces, accomplished in all the arts, a man of the most refined sensibility, delicacy of feeling, and deep emotional involvements, who plays a splendid role at a glittering court. But what he is not is just as revealing. Murasaki's hero has nothing of the moral stature or sense of princely/kingly duty that ennobles Rama in India. He is far removed from the sense of political and social responsibility that weighs on the Noble Man of Confucius and Mencius. Genji's heroic qualities are his brilliance as a dancer at court, as a painter, poet, and calligrapher. But Murasaki makes it clear that depth and delicacy of feeling is the true mark of the persons who command sympathy and admiration—if not official respect.

It is true that Murasaki's *Tale* is a work of the imagination, not a social document. It has often been pointed out that she and Sei Shonagon wrote in the Japanese vernacular and gave expression to Japanese sentiments, while formally educated Japanese men were writing in Chinese and affecting a role as Chinese literati. The world Murasaki and Shonagon described was the court as seen from the vantage point—and perhaps disadvantaged position—of court ladies.

Nevertheless the lack of reference to political issues in this court is not simply attributable to a disinterest or unawareness on the part of women writers. There was in fact little open political debate—matters of state were not public issues, but things decided behind the scenes through personal negotiation or manipulation. The consensus needed for action—or often inaction—was arrived at out of sight, if indeed there was any public watching the proceedings other than the insiders among the court nobility (*kuge*, literally "civil or public families") privy to these negotiations.

On the other hand, the aesthetic ideals and standards of proper conduct—often no less tacitly understood—were widely recognized as values shared by their age in general, as well as values formative of a classic sensibility that generations of Japanese later claimed for themselves. Granted then that Genji is a product of an aristocratic age and identifiable with a court nobility, we can differentiate his special quality from his classic Indian and Confucian counterparts by calling it "gentility"—the mark of a genteel culture, of aristocrats so privileged, so sustained within the workings of an hereditary class system, that they could enjoy the leisure just to be beautiful people.

That moral nobility was not a necessary feature of this gentility is also a reflection of prevailing religious tendencies. Shinto lacked a moral theology; it was governed by no

Mosaic law, church doctrine, or Confucian ethics. Instead, conduct was regulated by local custom, class status, and community consensus. "Good people" were well-bred members of a class wherein good manners and graceful conduct provided the standard of goodness. By the time Buddhism arrived in Japan, the ethical path originally identified with the noble Eightfold Path and the disciplinary precepts of the monastic code *(vinaya)* had been eroded by the tides of change in the Mahayana and the many concessions made through the practice of expedient means—in Japan more artful than moral.

Sometimes in the *Tale,* it is true, Genji is spoken of as greatly burdened by his past sins, and it is also true that in a widely influential religious tract of the same period, Genshin's (942–1017) *Essentials of Salvation,* as well as in popular art, people are vividly portrayed as suffering in hell for their sins. One must be careful, however, to recognize that sin here has a special meaning: it is more of an inveterate addiction or vice than a transgression against some divinely ordained law. It is a passionate attachment—in Buddhism often identified with the selfishness, self-indulgence, or self-willfulness of greed, anger, and passion—that stand as an impediment to one's liberation through the noble Eightfold Path. In other words, as the burden of self-incurred karma, it is more of a sin against oneself and one's realization of Buddhahood than a transgression of some objective moral order or fixed principle. And as convenient or expedient means became available for circumventing or by-passing the noble Eightfold Path to Enlightenment—for instance, taking the Easy Path of Pure Land, Buddhism's reliance on faith alone—sin in this sense became less of a burden, and in some cases it had a positive attraction—

"the passions as enlightenment" or love as leading to Buddhahood.

In Genji's particular case, his sinfulness has a special meaning for Murasaki, for it is the sinfulness of his passionate involvements and attachments—sometimes no more than indiscretions, at other times infatuations or obsessions—that both wound her deeply and attract her to him. What makes Genji her hero—and ennobles him in his very human condition—is precisely his capacity for deep feeling and passionate attachment. Such feelings move her too, and move her to write—in conscious awareness of their contradictoriness vis-à-vis the premises of Buddhism.[2]

An understanding of this point is key to a proper appreciation of the role of religion in the Heian period. Speaking of "The World of the Shining Prince" as represented in the work of Murasaki Shikibu and Sei Shonagon, Ivan Morris has said:

> Contemporary literature suggests that for many of the Heian aristocrats religion had become mere mummery. The temples may have been crowded with visitors, but the motives that brought them there often had little connection with the Buddhist faith. This is a subject that lends itself to satire and, as we might expect, no one has treated it more pungently than Sei Shonagon, whose mordant wit was, so far as we can judge, uninhibited by any deep religious feelings.[3]

If one understands the distance traveled by Buddhism from its beginnings as a world-renouncing religion (that is, religion understood as "leaving home and family") to one that, in the Mahayana, is in many respects world-accepting, one can appreciate the conflicted feelings of Sei Shonagon, who, far from being cynical, is quite conscious of the tension that exists between the worldly and other-worldly in the religion of her time, and understands that it would naturally express itself in a sense of conflict—a dis-harmony—between physical appearances and inner religi-osity.

Many passages in their works reveal the deep religious feelings of Murasaki and Shonagon and the difficulty they experience in reconciling the impulse toward world renun-ciation (going to a nunnery or going on retreat) and the aes-thetic and emotional attachments they are inclined to hold by the very adaptive (in Japan, aesthetic) means used to ex-press religion itself.

Shonagon was an inveterate participant in rituals and ceremonies at shrines, in temples, and at court. This pas-sage reports her feelings on revisiting the pilgrimage site at Hase Temple. It is one of the longest, most detailed ac-counts in the *Pillow Book,* and shows how much attention she actually gives to religion, though here, unfortunately, we must abridge it:

> On the way to our rooms we had to pass in front of rows of strangers. I found this very unpleasant; but, when I reached the chapel and got a view past the dog-barrier and right up to the sanctuary, I was overcome with awe and wondered how I could have stayed away for so many months. My old feelings were aroused and they overwhelmed all else. . . .
>
> Now, the bell rang for the recitation of the sutras. It was very comforting to think that it rang for me. In the cell next to ours a solitary gentleman was prostrating himself in prayer. At first I thought that he might be doing it because he knew we were listening; but soon I realized that he was absorbed in his devotions, which he continued hour after hour. I was greatly moved. When he rested from his prayers, he started reading the sutras in a loud, fervent voice. I was

wishing that he would read still more loudly so that I might hear every word; but instead he stopped and blew his nose—not in a noisy, unpleasant way but gently and discreetly. I wondered what he could be praying for so fervently and hoped that his wish might be granted. . . . Sometimes the booming of the temple bell became louder and louder until I was overcome with curiosity about who had asked for the readings. Then someone would mention the name of a great family, adding, "It is a service of instruction and guidance for Her Ladyship's safe delivery." An anxious period indeed, I thought, and would begin praying for the lady's well-being. . . .

The service continued all night, and it was so noisy that I could not get to sleep. After the matins I finally dozed off, only to be woken by a reading of the sutra consecrated to the temple Buddha. The priests were reciting loudly and raucously, without making any effort to sound solemn. From their tone I gathered that they were traveling monks and, as I listened to their voices which had awakened me so abruptly, I found myself being strangely moved.[4]

These are not the observations of someone "cynical" about religion, but rather of someone capable of deep religious feelings, at once aroused by sight and sound (the arts as "revealing the state of perfection," according to Kūkai), and at times distracted by these, but always hoping to re-experience the spiritual exaltation aroused by these encounters—all too dependent as these were on the momentary means of their excitement—and nostalgic for that past ecstatic moment.

The poignancy of Shonagon's situation is shown in her reference to the "loud" and "raucous" recitation of the monks, to which she reacted at first almost instinctively as coarse and boorish—far from the refined and elegant taste which her aestheticized culture had bred in this court lady as a kind of second nature. (Earlier in this account she had commented on the discomfort she felt on having to work her way through crowds of worshipers, presumably not of her class.) But in the end she acknowledges that she is "strangely moved" by the genuineness, the unaffected quality of the raffish monks' simple religiosity.

The obverse of her refined aestheticism, and its drawback, was the tendency prevalent among Heian aristocrats to be absorbed in their own genteel pursuits—the mark of their gentility—at the expense of a social conscience, moral sensibility, and above all, any sense of concern for the public good or general welfare. No doubt it was assumed that religious rituals, public processions, and impressive spectacles would suffice—that these would be edifying and inspiring enough for commoners.

If one were to look for a likely alternative to Murasaki's fictional hero Genji, or to Shonagon's exemplars of good taste—someone who might better qualify as representative of political culture in the Heian period—it would probably be Sugawara no Michizane (845–903), a scholar-statesman associated with an abortive attempt to reassert imperial authority and wrest some control away from the Fujiwaras. If he had been successful, his policies would have accommodated central control to the realities of growing local power exercised by provincial authorities; in other words, he would have recognized that the public domain, theoretically identified with the Imperial Court, had to be extended beyond the reach of the Fujiwara, and thus be shared with those who were gradually privatizing it themselves. But this was hardly an issue of public debate on the outcome of which Michizane's fate was to be determined. The Fujiwara, little concerned with public policy but successful in the largely unprincipled game of court politics, were able to recoup their position and personal control over the inner workings of the established system, and had Michizane sent into exile in Kyushu.

Michizane's eventual emergence as a cult hero was quite ironic. When unexpected personal misfortune struck the family of those responsible for his exile, it was attributed to the malevolence of Michizane's vengeful spirit, and shrines were erected to him (most famously, the Kitano Shintō Shrine in Kyoto), to appease his supposedly wrathful, vindictive spirit. Thus, as the cult of Michizane developed, it took the ambiguous form of observance to placate vengeful spirits on the one hand, and on the other, to celebrate Michizane as a paragon of learning and a patron deity, especially for those (in modern times) who would be taking entrance exams for schools, colleges, and official service.

As for Michizane's actual historic role, in no way connected with his role as a culture hero or Shinto deity, historians would more likely credit him with prescience in recognizing that the privatization of power in provincial hands had proceeded to the point where some realistic concessions would have to be made to it. The Fujiwara could not preserve forever their private monopoly of power as if they alone represented the public interest. The common terms applied to them, *kuge,* usually translated as "court nobility," was an oxymoron, *ku* standing for both public and noble, but *ge* for family; while the title they held, *kampaku* ("chancellor"), was commonly understood as "civil dictator." Now these euphemistic pretensions were coming undone.[5]

The eventual dissolution of the public sphere was formally recognized by the abandonment of key institutions of central control: the land distribution, tax collection system, and the state militia, originally modeled on similar institutions in Tang China and Shilla. By the end of the ninth century large private estates removed from the public domain had become the principal sources of income for both the Imperial house and court nobility—and, it is significant to note, for major temples and shrines as well. Thus the erosion of the public sphere (still nominally identified with the Kyoto court and court nobility) proceeded to the point where all major institutions—political, economic, military, and religious had been effectively privatized by the onset of the medieval period, thenceforth presided over, to the extent that this was possible at all in such circumstances, by the Kamakura and Ashikaga shogunates (military governments).

When Ruth Benedict, a cultural anthropologist, made her study of the Japanese in mid-twentieth century, she was unusually perceptive for her time in choosing the chrysanthemum and the sword to represent complementary aspects of the Japanese mentality. Instead of yielding to the prevailing caricatures of the Japanese as simply conflicted between a delicate aesthetic sensibility on the one hand, and a violent, aggressive militarism on the other, she saw the chrysanthemum as emblematic of a natural spontaneity, expressed typically in the art of flower-arranging, and the sword as an emblem of self-restraint—"not a symbol of aggression, but a simile of an ideal of self-responsible man."[6] Her seeing these two symbols as characteristic of the Japanese psyche in general is a warranted recognition of how deeply embedded these two cultural strains had become in the culture as a whole, even without an awareness on her part—understandable in a nonspecialist in things Japanese—of the depth of their historical significance. Since the chrysanthemum was also a particular symbol of the Imperial House, it can also be taken as emblematic of the high culture that flourished especially at the Heian Court and which left its mark on all Japanese of later years. The sword, on the other hand, was two-edged, and as a symbol of violence and cruelty (not just self-control) it too has a long history.

The stories of both the chrysanthemum and the sword could no doubt be traced back to the dawn of Japanese history; for our purposes, however, the emergence of the sword in medieval Japan, not just as a competitor or threat to the flower culture, but first as its foil and later even its accomplice, is a by-product of the flower culture's ascendancy at the Imperial Court itself. For the cultivation of a refined gentility and the aestheticization of the Heian Court—what might even be called its demoralization— brought the court's withdrawal from serious engagement with the project of building and maintaining the state as originally conceived by its founders—a universal state promoting the public good. Instead, the processes of privatization, already strong enough at the start to deflect the purposes of Prince Shōtoku, proceeded apace; and by the late twelfth century violence had overwhelmed gentility, the military coming to dominate the civil.

In medieval times the continuing importance of Kyoto as a center of high culture meant that even after the court's loss of political power to military forces, the court nobility and the religious establishment on Mount Hiei (interlocked with the former two) played a significant cultural/economic role because of their prestige and patronage in relation to the new arts and crafts production at the capital, and, as Kyoto grew economically, in connection with the new guilds of merchants and craftsmen. In the absence of any central public authority or source of political legitimization, the court and court nobility remained a factor in the cultural legitimization (through ritual and art) of power holders or pretenders to authority. All of this occurred within the general pattern of privatization, in which, as Jeffrey Mass has said, "Public authority came to be parceled out among the court and religious elite, gradually privatized, and thus shorn of part, but not all of its original legitimacy."[7] What remained, in the absence of any clear political or moral authority, was an aesthetic gentility that stood, along with certain historical and legal precedents, as a generally respected value.

When it came, the change to military control in the war of 1180–1185 was abrupt and shocking, and even if it had been long overdue as the inevitable result of the court's own workings, one could ask why, considering the seeming terminal weakness of the Heian regime, its end did not come sooner. Some of the answer lies in the fact that the court and court nobility were party to the process of privatization from the beginning, and it proceeded without direct challenge to or from them, while hardly anyone stood for the state as representing the public interest. But another reason for its staying power may be that, in spite of all, what this court was good for, it did well. Among a people who set a high value on art, beauty, and discriminating taste, the imperial chrysanthemum stood as a symbol of simple elegance; for this the Kyoto court was respected and continued to be so, long after power had gone. The chrysanthemum lived on, for Ruth Benedict and many others to admire, centuries later.

THE SWORD UNSHEATHED

The literature of the medieval period is replete with accounts of the violence and suffering that attended the rise to dominance of the warrior class as successors to the court nobility. Both the epic novels of the period and the Noh drama are pervaded by a sense of disaster, doom, and human tragedy, with the sudden downfall of elegant courtiers and heroic warriors as recurrent themes of the contemporary literature. One aspect of this is a nostalgia in violent times for the beautiful life, the peace and stability of the Heian Court, reflected in the literary meditations of Yoshida no Kenko, in his *Essays in Idleness* (*Tsurezuregusa,* c. 1330–32), which lament the decline in quality of the cultural life of the capital and the deterioration of the classic standards of taste. In the Noh play *Matsukaze,* the ghosts of two fisherwomen lament the loss of their erstwhile lover, the poet in exile Yukihira, who for a brief moment had brought the glory and beauty of the Heian Court into their drab and humble lives—a recollection too of Genji's exile in Suma. So also in the play *Komachi at Sekidera,* the Heian poetess Ono no Komachi is recalled both for her poetic gifts and captivating beauty, after she has lost both in her old age and is tormented by the shame of ugliness (not, we note, a moral fault, but an offense to the eye). Significantly, too, in a brief moment of release from her grief, Komachi relives, in a rapture of ecstatic dance, her past glory and affirms that poetry itself endures, even if all else human fails.

But perhaps the most touching moment in the warrior tales of the time is recounted in the *Tale of the Heike* (and then retold and reenacted again and again in the Noh

drama *Atsumori*). It involves the encounter and victory of
the Minamoto warrior, Kumagai, over a lone remnant of the
defeated Taira (Heike) clan, who for a few brief years had
occupied the capital and, in trying to live up to the standards of the court, had succumbed to its seductive gentility.
The *Tale* reads in part:

Kumagai no Jirō Naozane walked his horse toward the
beach after the defeat of the Heike. "The Taira nobles will
be fleeing to the water's edge in the hope of boarding rescue
vessels," he thought. "Ah, how I would like to grapple with a
high-ranking Commander-in-Chief!" Just then, he saw a
lone rider splash into the sea, headed toward a vessel in the
offing. The other was attired in crane-embroidered *neri-
nuki* silk *hitare,* a suit of armor with shaded green lacing
and a horned helmet. At his waist, he wore a sword with gilt
bronze fittings; on his back, there rode a quiver containing arrows fledged with black-banded white eagle feathers.
He grasped a rattan-wrapped bow and bestrode a white-
dappled reddish horse with a gold-edged saddle. When his
mount had swum out about a hundred and fifty or two hundred feet, Naozane beckoned with his fan.

"I see that you are a Commander-in Chief. It is dishonor-
able to show your back to an enemy. Return!"

The warrior came back. As he was leaving the water,
Naozane rode up alongside him, gripped him with all his
strength, crashed with him to the ground, held him motion-
less and pushed aside his helmet to cut off his head. He was
sixteen or seventeen years old, with a lightly powdered face
and blackened teeth—a boy just the age of Naozane's own
son Kojirō Naoie, and so handsome that Naozane could not
find a place to strike.

"Who are you? Announce your name. I will spare you,"
Naozane said.

"Who are you?" the youth asked.

"Nobody of any importance: Kumagai no Jirō Naozane, a resident of Musashi Province."

"Then it is unnecessary to give you my name. I am a desirable opponent for you. Ask about me after you take my head. Someone will recognize me, even if I don't tell you."

"Indeed, he must be a Commander-in-Chief," Naozane thought. "Killing this one person will not change defeat into victory, nor will sparing him change victory into defeat. When I think of how I grieved when Kojirō suffered a minor wound, it is easy to imagine the sorrow of this young lord's father if he were to hear that the boy had been slain. Ah, I would like to spare him!" Casting a swift glance to the rear, he discovered Sanehira and Kagetoki coming along behind him with fifty riders.

"I would like to spare you," he said, restraining his tears, "but there are Genji warriors everywhere. You cannot possibly escape. It will be better if I kill you than if someone else does, because I will offer prayers on your behalf."

"Just take my head and be quick about it."

Overwhelmed by compassion, Naozane could find no place to strike. His senses reeled, his wits forsook him and he was scarcely conscious of his surroundings. But matters could not go on like that forever; in tears, he took the head.

"Alas! No lot is as hard as a warrior's. I would never have suffered such a dreadful experience if I had not been born into a military house. How cruel I was to kill him." He pressed his sleeve to his face and shed floods of tears.

Presently, since matters could not go on like that forever, he started to remove the youth's armor *hitatare* so that he might wrap it around the head. A brocade bag containing a flute was tucked in at the waist. "Ah, how pitiful! He must have been one of the people I heard making music inside the stronghold just before dawn. There are tens of thousands of riders in our eastern armies, but I am sure none of them has brought a flute to the battlefield. Those court nobles are refined men!"

When Naozane's trophies were presented for Yoshitsune's inspection, they drew tears from the eyes of all the beholders. It was learned later that the slain youth was, Tayū Atsumori, aged seventeen, a son of Tsunemori, the Master of the Palace Repairs Office.

After that, Naozane thought increasingly of becoming a monk.[8]

In the pathos of this episode is the quintessential paradox of the feudal age: an outpouring of Buddhist compassion, overridden by the stern code of war in this hero, fatefully "born into a military household" and thus undeterred by Buddhism's prohibition of killing.

Indeed, in these violent and unpredictable times, it was individual honor, however construed, that remained the only absolute value. To the extent that any external restraint availed, it could be found in the bonds of feudal obligation and the codes of the military governments and military households, themselves representing a privatization of law after the lapse of any public order.

The adoption of feudal codes proceeded, like so many changes of the medieval period, by indirection and default. It was left to the Hojo regents—acting supposedly on behalf of Kamakura shoguns, themselves acting supposedly for the Emperor, to take upon themselves the task of legislation governing feudal personal relations and establish standards of fairness in settling disputes. This occurred without any overt challenge to the law codes of the Nara and Heian period, which simply stood where they were, largely unchanged. When reference to them had to be made, the interested parties consulted a few families in the old capital which did not themselves make policy or administer the law.

The contents of the Jōei Code promulgated by Hōjō Yasutoki (1193–1242) had to do primarily with warriors, the duties and authority of the constables and stewards serving the shogunate, inheritance rights, and so forth. The later Kenmu Code of the Ashikaga shogunate further recognized the need for regulating the conduct of vassals, but evoked the precedent of Shōtoku's Constitution, appealing thereby to some residual sense of fair standards and common justice, and in this respect to some consideration of merit in appointments—anomalous in view of the fact that most positions were held on the basis of birth into powerful families. Intriguing too is the provision that would prevent "powerful courtiers, women and Zen monks from meddling in government" (SJT I, 419).

In the Muromachi period (1336–1573) there was a further loosening of the shogun's control over the local feudal powers (the *daimyō,* literally "great names," again suggesting the privatization of power), and the problem persisted of how, in these almost anarchic circumstances, any common standards could be applied or some general authority be upheld. Thus in the house codes promulgated by the daimyo there was a need not only to deal with relations among vassals but also to curb the excesses of free-booting and personal vendettas among the samurai. Indeed, given the flexibility of moral means in this age, a serious problem arose from the tendency to put personal honor ahead even of loyalty to the lord—a matter difficult to deal with since the appeal to "honor" went beyond practical self-interest.

The term had an almost religious intensity—as if the issue of personal honor overrode all other values and interests, transcending the otherwise expedient morality that tended to prevail, even in matters of feudal loyalty. A lasting and powerful vestige of this was the act of suicide as the ultimate, redeeming demonstration of personal honor, a practice which eventually spread well beyond the samurai class itself.

Of more direct concern to the shogunate in the cult of honor was the associated belief in the right of self-redress, vengeance, and personal vendetta (the forming of bands of warriors to exact redress for an affront or insult) which could often conflict with the interests of the daimyo in maintaining some kind of unity and stability. It was partly in response to this conflict that the countervailing insistence on "loyalty to one's lord" emerged as a prime demand on the samurai conscience attempting to rein in the samurai's independence.

Given the decentralization of the feudal system as well as the wide range and heterogeneous character of the personal problems to be dealt with in the local or family setting, much of the contents of the House Laws (kahō) or Family Instructions (kakun) consisted of general prudential advice, promoting the virtues of simplicity, frugality, and self-sufficiency, which became hallmarks of the samurai lifestyle. In this connection, we note an intriguing case of extravagance that betrays the weakness even of the samurai for the aesthetic indulgences of the Muromachi Court in Kyoto. In the Seventeen Article Household Code of Asakura Toshikage (a leading vassal of the Ashikagas), which consciously evoke Shōtoku's Constitution, among the extravagances enjoined against (in addition to fancy dress, fine horses, falcons for hunting) there are two revealing stipulations:

5. We should not eagerly invite troops of the four schools of *sarugaku*[9] down from Kyoto for the pleasure of viewing them. With the money saved, we could select talented people from our domain, send them to Kyoto for dance training and take pleasure in them ever after.
6. There will be no performances of *Noh* at night within the fort precincts.

Obviously the lure of Kyoto's high culture, in the up-to-date form of the *Noh* drama, extended even to the countryside, among coarse and brutish warriors.

During the sixteenth century, the attempt to establish law and order through the house laws of the leading daimyo was mostly directed at the warrior class, and at settling disputes and vendettas among them that drained resources away from what the daimyo saw as central to their own interests. In trying to assert their own superior authority over the conflicting private interests of samurai, the daimyo, in their house laws, invoked Shōtoku's old ideal of "public authority" *(kōgi)*, claiming to speak for the general good and to legitimize their own power after the default of the old Imperial Court, whose vestigial claim to authority, still formally acknowledged, rested mainly on its residual cultural prestige.

One could wish for some one word that would convey all the facets of samurai mentality and express the dominant spirit of this medieval culture—in contrast to the classic gentility of the Imperial Capital and Court. Though the daimyo and samurai constitute a new aristocracy, it is a question whether their characteristic value could be spoken of as nobility, if we have the high moral ideals of King Rama or the civil leadership role of the Confucian Noble Man in mind, "Chivalry," of course, suggests itself in connection with the samurais' demanding code of honor. Here too, however, there are obvious incongruities with the Western type—courtliness, especially towards women, is often thought a mark of chivalry in the West, but is absent here. At the same time, although courtliness and civility seem to be natural antitheses of the warrior's constant resort to force, the house laws themselves encourage civility in the form of respect for elders, for learning, and for poetry— alongside maxims more typical of a warrior-driven expedience, like "Call the warrior a dog, call him a beast: winning is his business!"[10] Lastly, the cult of suicide as the supreme test of honor and integrity in the code of the samurai would find no counterpart in the chivalry of the Christian West, with its divine sanction against suicide, as in Prince Hamlet's deference to the Almighty's having "fixed his canon against self-slaughter."

The devolution of central authority and the crescendo of violence, brutality, and treachery in Japan reached a climax in the period known as Sengoku (1478–1568), which can mean "the country at war" or "the warring states"—a period riven by internal strife, but not perhaps to be understood as "civil war" if by that one means the rupture of a civil union—since none such had existed for centuries. The memory of an earlier unified order did persist, however, and could serve as a measure of legitimate rule (emperors who reigned but did not rule being something else).

In a period known for "subordinates overthrowing superiors" (gekokujō), the inferiors contending for power tried to offset the violence marking their way to the top, as well as their often questionable ethics, by invoking the ideal of unity under the aegis of Heaven as a validating principle. In this situation religion did not serve well as a unifying force. Major temples and shrines, as well as new religious communities, were armed camps or even powerful fortresses defending their own interest in the general contention among rival forces. Sectarianism arose from the tendency of new Buddhist movements to emphasize exclusive allegiance to particular objects of worship, texts, or practices, and then from the need to defend themselves against the reprisals of the establishment or the rival claims of others to exclusive loyalties. Mount Hiei and the Tendai organization were still universalistic in theory and in their receptivity to diverse practices, both exoteric and esoteric, but in organization and direction they had largely become privatized under the hereditary leadership of Fujiwara branch houses. Meanwhile, as traditional discipline yielded to lay devotional practices, with celibacy largely abandoned, the leadership of many religions and temples too became hereditary. In religions emphasizing faith and direct personal enlightenment, merit no longer counted; there was then no obstacle to the general Japanese proclivity toward inherited headship—blood succession (ketsu-myaku sōjō) rather than spiritual or moral qualification (hō-myaku sōjō).

A good illustration of how this adaptation to circumstances tended to fill the void left in the moral sphere is the controversy regarding the monk Hōnen's exclusive, unqualified devotion to Amida Buddha in the True Pure Land Sect. More traditional defenders of Buddhism like Jōkei (1153–1213) and Myōe (1173–1232) censured Hōnen for his abandonment of the standard disciplinary precepts. Jōkei, reaffirming the established view of Buddhism as protecting the state through the spiritual benefits accruing from the practice of Buddhism, deplored the failure of Hōnen to uphold its disciplines.[11] For both Hōnen and his critics, however, it was a question not of how these precepts related to the political or social order, but of how necessary they were to the attaining of religious salvation.

By the time of Rennyo (1415–1499), later head of the True Pure Land sect, the internalization and privatization of religious experience through personal faith and trust in Amida alone, and through exclusive practice devoted to one single object of worship (*honzon*), had become privatized also on the social level by the organization of sects (no longer just different schools of an inclusive Mahayana universalism) which took on increasingly the feudal character of medieval Japan. The hereditary succession to religious leadership in Japan, in contrast to Buddhist succession by spiritual merit, is one indication of this. But the need for Rennyo to adapt to the situation in his time also took the form of setting rules for governing his lay religious community. There might be no need for discipline or the acquisition of merit as a matter of religious salvation—as if one's after-life depended on it—but there was indeed a need to have rules for the survival of the lay religious community, as if the present life depended on it. Thus Rennyo tried to come to terms with the actual state of affairs facing him, including the prevailing contentiousness among the religious sects, while keeping to some minimal observance of lay Buddhist practice. In general, he sought to avoid provocation of other sects and conflict with the feudal authorities, while carefully guarding his sect's own religious identity. Thus at the end of his rules, Rennyo demands that his followers "should expel from your assembly any people who turn their backs on these regulations." In so ostracizing nonconformists, Rennyo demonstrates how exclusivity has become privatized beyond individual religious practice, to a sectarian privatization in the social sphere as well.[12]

As the court had become privatized and religion no longer plausibly served to protect a state, religious communities themselves became fragmented and dependent on their own resources, which, in a militarized country, meant the arming of monasteries, temples, shrines, and faith communities for their own defense. A faint echo persisted of the earlier idea that Buddhism and the state should be protective of each other, heard in the Zen master Eisai's (1141–1215) tract "Promote Zen for the Protection of the State." Eisai's emphasis, however, was on the promotion of Zen itself, assuming (as of old) that this would redound to the moral and spiritual benefit of any ruling patron; he did not suggest that Zen had any public morality or political program to offer. By contrast, the monk Nichiren (1227–1282), intolerant of any but his own belief, severely criticized the Pure Land and Zen sects for abandoning the state, in the former case for their exclusive attention to Amida and the Pure Land ("One Buddha, One Mind/ Heart, One Direction"), and in the latter case for Zen practice, which Nichiren considered self-centered and detracting from any public service to the nation. Nichiren himself, however, though intensely nationalistic, was no less exclusive in his devotion to the *Lotus Sutra* as a spiritual panacea, and he devoted much of his strident proselytization to attacking the ruling shoguns and regents for betraying the nation by failing to honor the Lotus and Japan's native Shinto gods.

The Zen sect, which Eisai imported from China, did indeed show some versatility by adapting itself to a wide range of separate purposes: those of the Imperial Court, court nobility, shoguns, and daimyos. Zen monks established themselves too in a variety of roles and enterprises: as Imperial chaplains, official advisers to shoguns, mentors to samurai in the martial arts, entrepreneurs in the China trade, landscape architects, designers of tea houses—everything from the military arts to the aesthetic. In thus serving the military leadership, as well as the surviving elite of the aesthetic culture patronized by the Muromachi court in Kyoto, Zen monks played an important role in what is known as the Higashiyama culture so formative of the later Japanese aesthetic tradition. Thus they demonstrated their ability to bridge the dominant military and aesthetic trends of the time, but not the political divisions that left the country at war.

Indeed, during the problematic rule of Ashikaga Yoshimasa (1436–1490), the predominance of an aesthetic culture over a political one contributed to major losses in the shogun's control of power, even while Yoshimasa established himself as a prominent patron and practitioner of the arts which characterized the Higashiyama culture—new styles of painting, calligraphy, ceramics, flower-arranging, teahouses, tea ceremony, the Noh plays, the comic interludes in Noh performances (*kyōgen*), garden design and landscape architecture, and so forth. Often informed by the Zen spirit, these arts were characterized by an aesthetic of studied nonchalance, casualness, off-handedness, and a noncommittal attitude that has also been called "disinterestedness"—a pragmatic adaptability that easily accommodated itself to the prevailing decline in political morality. By now the public sphere had virtually collapsed, and legitimacy was measured, not by civil values, but by such aesthetic gentility and refinement as could be appropriated even by military men. Violence itself thereby became dignified, and a mystique of war and violence joined the gentle arts to the Way of the Warrior. With this virile legacy lasting down to the twentieth century, in World War II kamikaze suicide pilots fell like cherry blossoms on land and sea.

The classic expression of this aesthetic mystique of the warrior is found in the *Hagakure* (In the Shadow of Leaves) by the Zen master Yamamoto Tsunetomo (1657–1719). In a work that became a powerful inspiration for the militarism of late nineteenth and twentieth century Japan, Yamamoto expounded his view of a beautiful death:

> I have found that the Way of the Samurai is death. This means that when you are compelled to choose between life and death, you must quickly choose death. . . .
>
> Until fifty or sixty years ago, samurai would take a bath every morning, put scent onto the shaven part of the head and into their hair, cut their nails, file them with a pumice stone and polish them with oxalis, and pay very careful attention to their personal appearance. They would be especially careful to see that all of their weapons and armor were free of rust, wiping away all dust and dirt and polishing them up so they were always ready for use. To take great pains over one's appearance may seem to be merely adorning the external, but it is not just some kind of affectation of elegance. It was because they were always in a state of preparedness, thinking, "Today I might die in battle. If I were to be killed in battle with a sloppy appearance, my lack of preparedness in ordinary times would be revealed, and I would be looked upon contemptuously by the enemy as a slovenly fellow." Thus, whether a samurai was young or old,

he would always give careful attention to his physical appearance. Certainly it is troublesome and it takes time, but this is what the work of the samurai is. . . .

A samurai who is not always prepared to die at any moment without regret will inevitably end up dying an unbecoming death. . . .

It is awful if a samurai's mind gets stuck on judgments of right and wrong, whether something is loyal or disloyal, righteous or unrighteous, proper or improper, and so on. If one just devotes oneself totally and single-mindedly to the service of one's lord, forgetting all other considerations, and cherishes one's lord without second or third thoughts, that is enough.

The text shows a strong continuity between the medieval mentality of the Ashikaga samurai and a modern writer like Mishima Yukio (1925–1970) (see Chapter 8), but in the intervening period this same view is found among the warriors prominent in the sixteenth-century reunification of Japan and the subsequent invasion of Korea by the Japanese. Yamamoto quotes a leading general in the latter invasion, Nabeshima Naoshige (1538–1618), as epitomizing this attitude in the saying: "Bushidō is nothing but charging forward into death." And Yamamoto comments: "In a normal state of mind, you cannot accomplish a great task. You must become like a person crazed. . . . As soon as discriminating thoughts arise, you will already have fallen behind."[13]

UNITY AND LEGITIMACY

The warlord Oda Nobunaga, the first of those who subsequently strove to achieve unity in sixteenth-century Japan, is counted as from a "priestly family" (an expression that in itself betrays the privatization of religion as compared to the earlier idea of religious life as "leaving home and family"), but was little restrained by Buddhist professions about peace and the sparing of life. In his rise to power he found himself opposed by the militant monks of the Enryakuji temple on Mount Hiei, and when victorious, he burned to the ground the many temple buildings on the mountain and ruthlessly slaughtered all of their inhabitants. As he was no paragon of ethical sensitivity, it is not surprising that at the height of his power he was assassinated through the treachery of one of his own lieutenants.

Some small indication of the man's bloodthirstiness shows up in a letter to one of his vassals:

> In the town of Fuchū itself we took as many as one and a half thousand heads, and in the environs we took in all two thousand more. We killed three ranking captains: Saikōji. Shimotsuma Izumi, and Wakabayashi. . . . The town of Fuchū is nothing but corpses, with not a clear spot anywhere around; I'd like to show it to you! Today I shall search every mountain and every valley, and I shall kill them all.[14]

And in another follow-up letter he reports:

> After smashing the enemy defenses at Kinome and Hachibuse and decapitating Saikōji, Shimotsuma Izumi Hokkyō, and Wakabayashi as well as Toyohara Saihōin, Asakura Saburō and their ilk, I divided the troops into four contingents and had them search every mountain and every valley without exception, cutting heads. On the 17th, more than two thousand heads were delivered; seventy or eighty were taken alive, so their heads were cut off. On the 18th, five or six hundred heads at a time arrived from vari-

ous places, quite impossible to tell how many in all. . . .
Shibata Shuri no Suke and Korezumi Gorōzaemon no Jō attacked and destroyed the stronghold held by Asakura Yozō. They killed more than six hundred men of standing; more than a hundred were taken alive, so their heads were cut off. On the 20th I sent [Sakuma] Kuemon no Jō, Maeda Matazaemon, as well as men of the Horse Guards to a mountain called Hinagatake, where they cut down more than a thousand. More than a hundred were taken alive, so their heads too were chopped off. (449)

The account continues at great length and in much gruesome detail but the following lines may suffice to show Nobunaga's utter lack of compassion: "It was previously reported that Shimotsuma Chikugo had been driven into a river; actually, he was making his way to Kazao, supporting himself on a bamboo cane and wearing a bamboo hat. An individual loyal to me cut off his head. When it was delivered here, I must say I relished the sight" (450).

All the same, to justify his ruthless conquests and undercut the shogunal authority he was usurping, Nobunaga faults the last of the Ashikaga shoguns for his failure to observe the niceties of proper decorum in serving the Emperor (this was the nominal function of a shogun), and in choosing an improper era name for the Emperor's reign. In the process of detailing other evidences of the shogun's misfeasance and gaucheness, Nobunaga manages to claim that these derelictions of the shogun have become "the talk of the entire realm," that is, "all-under-Heaven," as if Nobunaga spoke for the people and the people for Heaven. There was then still some theoretical court of appeal: Heaven as the moral authority under the aegis of which the court was still supposed to conduct its affairs. And in an age marked by the privatization of power, might made right but still in the name of Heaven.

Toyotomi Hideyoshi (1537–1598), successor to Nobunaga in the process of unification, was only slightly less bloodthirsty than Nobunaga (preferring sieges to direct assault), but still left a monument to his cruel exploits in Korea, where the trophies collected by his invading troops took the form of, not heads as with Nobunaga, but the ears and noses of slain Koreans, collected and sent back to what legendarily became known as the Mound of Ears *(mimizuka)* in Kyoto's Higashiyama district, near Amida Peak where he was buried (hoping for salvation in the Pure Land!) The Mound of Ears was not far from other monuments to Hideyoshi's glory: the Toyokuni [Hōkoku] Shinto Shrine in Kyoto, according him divine status, and the great Buddha figure constructed to rival if not outdo Emperor Shōmu's Daibutsu in Nara.

Hideyoshi's attempts to legitimize himself did not stop with his appropriation of symbols and rituals of Buddhism and Shinto, nor would he have been satisfied by simply taking over the somewhat discredited office of shogun. A commoner with no aristocratic pedigree—indeed so low-born that he did not even possess a family surname—Hideyoshi did his best to equip himself with all the trappings of the old court nobility, including the title of civil dictator *(kampaku)* or Senior Regent *(taikō)*, as if to distinguish himself by identification with the civil nobility the Fujiwara were believed to represent. Even his invasion of Korea, aiming at conquest of China, was done in the name of the Japanese emperor, through whose prestige Hideyoshi sought to gain access to the highest sources of political legitimation. To this end he also arranged an elaborate reception for the

Emperor at which court officials and daimyo swore undying loyalty to the throne.

Beyond this Hideyoshi tried to assume the mantle of Heian-style patron of the arts, outdoing himself with extravaganzas in the performance of a mammoth tea ceremony and as sponsor of poetry readings, Noh performances, and an enormous flower-viewing ceremony—attempting to gain prestige from patronage precisely of those genteel arts which, under the Ashikaga, had succeeded to and reenlivened the aesthetic culture so identified with the Fujiwara brand of civility—the gentility of the Heian court which had become the Japanese replacement for Shōtoku's projected civil state.

Hideyoshi's power rested on a foundation of feudal relations—a network of personal ties that preserved the privatized power system which had evolved over the centuries. Thus, although he enacted several measures that were intended to assert greater control over the country—the regulation of commerce, confiscation of arms, the compilation of a land survey and population register, and measures to tighten fiscal and social controls—Hideyoshi's death, premature in regard to the completion of his civil and military ambitions, left him without an heir firmly in place, but only with an infant son, presumably protected by a regency council consisting of vassals and allies in the loose confederation he had been able to form. But feudal loyalties being the "sometime thing" of the sixteenth century, with its flexible, expedient morality, it was not long before Hideyoshi's designated heir had been overthrown by one of his own supposed guardians, Tokugawa Ieyasu (1543–1616).

Ieyasu, a more methodical planner and careful manager than Hideyoshi, succeeded in unifying Japan on a more stable basis under a system that has been characterized as "centralized feudalism"—in other words, under a military shogunate with better control over the daimyo, but with these feudal domains intact and the samurai still an hereditary, military aristocracy. Continuity with the feudal past is further shown by Ieyasu's recourse to legislation in the form and genre of the medieval house laws, enacting regulations to ensure against any possible power alignment that might threaten the dominance of his own "military headquarters" *(bakufu)*. In this process he even dictated regulations for the Imperial Court and nobility (the *kuge*) that kept them occupied with the rituals and genteel arts, leaving governance to the *bakufu*.

Instead of continuing Hideyoshi's ostentatious patronage of the Imperial Court and the aesthetic culture in Kyoto —which, in the absence of real power, still embodied the civil aspect of imperial rule—Ieyasu looked elsewhere for legitimation. Without abandoning his connections to the Buddhist establishment (he kept three advisers from the Tendai, Pure Land, and Zen sects), he looked for possible help from spokesmen for the Neo-Confucian movement that had extended itself, by this time, to much of East Asia. That development proved to be a major one in Japan, and while this is not the place to recount it, one early encounter between Ieyasu and the ex-Zen monk and convert to Neo-Confucianism, Hayashi Razan (1635–1657), will serve to highlight the issue of legitimation, which still survived from the time of Prince Shōtoku down through successive stages in the devolution of the public sphere Shōtoku had once projected.

In an interview between Ieyasu and Razan, recorded in the latter's "Answer to Questions of the Bakufu" [that is,

Ieyasu], Ieyasu raised a fundamental question concerning legitimacy, including whether there is such a thing as right and wrong—a question Shōtoku had already raised in his Constitution from the standpoint of Mahayana "Emptiness," which is Non-dualist but relativistic in regard to moral judgments. In those terms the Mean transcends all dichotomies of right and wrong, and is arrived at through a process of thoroughgoing negation (the Middle Way), while Razan's conception of the Mean derives from the Chinese philosopher Zhu Xi's conception of the Mean as representing the common good or public good.

In the following episode Ieyasu questions whether the Confucian Way has ever been successfully practiced in China, and whether even the sage-kings Wen and Wu did not have to use force in coming to power. Implied is the question of what is legitimate discretion and what is expediency in the practical implementation of the Way.

Ieyasu said to Dōshun [Razan's Buddhist name]: "The Way has never been practiced, neither now, nor formerly. Therefore, [in the *Zhongyong*] it says 'The course of the Mean cannot be attained' and 'The path of the Mean is untrodden.' What do you think of this?" Dōshun answered: "The Way *can* be practiced. What the *Zhongyong* says is, I think, something that Confucius said when he was complaining of the fact that the Way was not being practiced. It does not mean that the Way cannot actually be practiced. In the Six Classics there are many lamentations like this. It is not only in the *Zhongyong*."

Ieyasu asked what was meant by "the Mean" [or Middle; *zhong* in Chinese; *chū* in Japanese]. I answered: "The Mean (or Middle) is difficult to grasp. The middle of one foot is not the middle of one *jō* (3 meter/10 yard/1 fathom).

The middle of a room is not the middle of a house. The middle of a state is not the middle of the empire. All things have their own Middle. Only when you have grasped their principle, can you say that you have found their Middle [Mean]. However much they want to know the Mean, those who have only just begun their studies can never obtain it, precisely because they do not know the principles. For this reason we have the maxim, valid now and formerly, that 'the Mean is nothing but Principle.'"

Ieyasu said: "In both the Middle [Way] and Expediency there can be good or bad. Tang [in overthrowing the last king of Xia] and Wu [in overthrowing the last king of Shang] were vassals who overthrew their lords. Their actions, though bad, were good. As the phrase goes, 'In taking the empire they went against the Way, and in keeping it, they followed the Way.' Therefore, 'neither good nor bad' is the ultimate truth of the Middle [Way]."

I answered: "My opinion is different from this. May I be allowed to speak my mind? I think that the Mean is good, that it does not have one speck of evil. The Mean is, that you attain the principles of all things and that your every action accords with the standard of rightness. If one regards the good as good and uses it, and regards evil as evil and shuns it, that is also the Mean. If one knows what is correct and incorrect and distinguishes between what is heterodox and orthodox, this is also the Mean. Tang and Wu followed Heaven and reacted to the wishes of mankind. They never had one particle of egoistic desires. On behalf of all-under Heaven [the people of the empire] they removed a great evil. How can that be 'good, though bad?' The actions of Tang and Wu were in accord with the Mean; they are instances of [legitimate] discretion. The case is quite different from that of the usurper Wang Mang [33 BCE–23 CE], who overthrew the Former Han dynasty, or of Cao Cao [155–

220], who was responsible for the fall of the Latter Han dynasty. They were nothing but brigands. As for the phrase that 'In taking the empire they went against the Way and in keeping it they followed the Way'—this [moral relativism] is applicable only to actions such as lies, deceit and opportunistic plotting.[15]

Here Ieyasu proposes a relativistic standard of good and evil, citing the Madhyamika Buddhist doctrine that the Middle Way of Supreme Wisdom lies in adhering to neither good nor evil. Razan responds that the Confucian Mean, in contrast to the Buddhist Middle Way of non-discrimination, consists in making value judgments and acting on behalf of the common good; by so doing one achieves unity with the Way. Ieyasu cites the historic examples of Cheng Tang overthrowing the last king of Xia, and King Wu of Zhou overthrowing the last ruler of Shang, as cases of expediency. Razan views these as cases of legitimate discretion in acting for the Way. Thus the argument here hinges on the double meaning of the term *quan*, (Japanese *ken*), understood by Ieyasu as "expediency" and by Razan as the legitimate exercise of discretion. The former emphasizes moral ambiguity; the latter the need to resolve the ambiguity by judgments on behalf of the common good.

On the twenty-fifth day of the sixth month the *bakufu* said to Dōshun: . . . "What is that so-called 'Unity that pervades all?'" Dōshun answered: "The heart of the Sage is nothing but Principle. Now, always and everywhere, Principle runs through all things and all actions in the world; the Sage reacts to them and acts on them according to this unitary Principle. . . . To give an example, it is like the movement of spring, summer, fall and winter, or warm and cold, day and night: though they are not identical, yet they are a cyclical stream of one and the same original matter that is not disrupted for one single moment. For that reason actions in the world may be ten-, hundred-, thousand- or ten-myriadfold, but that by which the mind-and-heart reacts to them is only the one, unitary Principle. With one's lord it is [manifested as] loyalty; with one's father, as filial piety; with one's friends, as trust; but none of these Principles is different in origin."

The *bakufu* again said: "Were the wars of Tang and Wu instances of discretion or expediency?" Dōshun answered: "The purpose of the actions of Tang and Wu was not to acquire the empire for themselves, but only to save the people."[16]

In this discussion the terms Ieyasu uses are familiar ones in Mahayana Buddhist philosophy, but those used by Hayashi Razan are sometimes derived from Neo-Confucianism, terms such as "principle" and "unitary principle," which have a new meaning as part of the conceptual language developed in Song and Ming China. Razan's point is clear enough: the ruler can legitimize himself by using his power to benefit the people. All Ieyasu has to do in order to legitimize himself is to do right. But to appreciate fully what this means for civility and the new civil discourse that would attempt to turn feudal Japan into a civil society in the Tokugawa period (1600–1868), we must turn back to earlier developments in Song China.

6

The New Leadership and Civil Society in Song China

When Hayashi Razan responded to Tokugawa Ieyasu's question whether "legitimacy" amounted to anything more than simple expediency, Razan spoke of moral values—right and wrong—and human moral relations as grounded in the very structure and processes of Heaven-and-Earth, corresponding to the natural order as seen in the succession of the seasons. For this Razan was drawing on a new Confucian metaphysics and cosmology known to the Japanese by this time as "Song Learning," identifying it as a product of a long development in and out of Song period China (907–1126).

The circumstances which gave rise to it at the end of the Tang and Five Dynasties periods resemble in significant ways the historical situation of Ieyasu and Razan. The centralized state of the early Tang, so admired by Korea and Japan earlier, had been seriously weakened and military warlords had taken overmuch of its power. Contemporary scholarly concern over this dynastic weakness took at least two forms of long-term significance: one was a new interest in the historical study of civil institutions with a view to restoring the strength of the state, exemplified by Tu Yu's (735–812) encyclopedic *Comprehensive Institutions (Tong-dian);* the other was Han Yü's protest against the Imperial Court's acceptance of the mystique of rulership implicit in its sponsorship of Buddhist rituals. Han Yü rejected a popular syncretism of his day, which saw the Three Teachings (Confucianism, Daoism, and Buddhism) as One and emphasized their complementarity.

In his essay "On the Way," Han Yü insisted that the Confucian Way was distinct from Daoism and Buddhism; it represented the values of civilization, as the others did not. Buddhism had the additional defect of being a foreign religion, but his pairing of it with native Daoism showed that the underlying issue was cultural and not ethnic.

To love largely is called humaneness; to act according to what should be done is called rightness. To proceed from these principles is called the Moral Way *(Dao):* to be sufficient unto oneself without depending on externals is called virtue. . . . Thus there is the Way of the Noble Man and the way of the inferior person. . . .

Laozi belittled humaneness and rightness; he disparaged and spoke ill of them. Yet his view was limited. . . . Laozi divorces humaneness and rightness from the Way and virtue. . . . But this is only the private opinion of one man. . . .

In ancient times men confronted many dangers. But sages arose who taught them the way to live and grow together. They served as rulers and teachers. . . . The people were cold and they clothed them, hungry and they fed them. Because people dwelt in trees and fell to the ground, dwelt in caves and became ill, the sages built houses for them. They fashioned crafts so people could provide themselves with implements. . . .

But now Buddhist doctrine maintains that one must reject the relationship between ruler and minister and do away with father and son; they ban the Way that enables us to live and grow together—all this in order to seek what they call purity and nirvana.[1]

Here Han Yü affirms key elements of the Confucian Way that would later characterize the Confucian revival in the Song era: the Confucian Way as a moral Way based on human relationships, and also as the Way of the Noble Man and the sage-king, who are leaders in sustaining human life and helping people to flourish in civilized society. In so emphasizing the leadership role of the sage-king, however, Han Yü outdid himself. He cast the ruler in a strong authoritarian role, and in one of his long poems engaged in egregious hero-worship of the reigning emperor (574). This was not to be typical of later Confucian thought as a whole, but it did betray a besetting temptation, and sometimes an actual sin, of those who, in attempting to have rulers emulate the sage-kings, ended up persuading them they were such.

As it brought unity to China after a prolonged period of warlordism, the Song dynasty sought to establish a strong civil society. For this purpose they resurrected and greatly strengthened the civil service, and they promoted the kind of scholarship that would be useful in civil administration. The encyclopedic Imperial Conspectus of Great Peace (*Taiping yulan*) provided an anthology of writings on institutional history that would be useful to rulers and civil officials.

When one speaks of "civil society" in the Song era, one does so in the context of the historical situation at that time, not according to some modern European definition. Here we refer to a new emphasis on civil rule as opposed to military, to a new civil official class (in contrast to administration by an old aristocracy and subsequent warlordism) serving in a meritocratic civil service system and prepared for that service through a new system of education and examination. Other circumstances contributed to this development—a growing economy, an expanding commercial class, greater affluence and leisure for cultural pursuits, and technological developments like the spread of printing, which enabled wider literacy and education. But the uses these new developments would be put to reflected new movements in thought, concurrent efforts at economic, social, and political reform, and eventually a new philosophy and ideology that would outlive the circumstances of their original creation.

Not surprisingly, the new reformist thought involved a reformulation of the earlier concept of the Noble Man or Person, *junzi,* central to classic Confucian thought. A leading statesman of the eleventh century, Fan Zhongyan, memorably characterized the Confucian Noble Person as "First in worrying about the world's worries and last in enjoying its pleasures." Fan's language comes directly from Mencius (1A:2) when the sage urged King Hui of Liang to share his pleasures with the people, and also when he spoke about the need for anyone who became aware of people's needs or the dangers facing them, to warn those slower and later in coming to such an awareness. At least one modern commentator has suggested that this was a Song adaptation of the Mahayana Buddhist ideal of the bodhisattva as a savior figure, and although the language of the epigram is thoroughly Mencian, it is plausible to think that what elicited it in the Song situation and what gave it such relevance to the contemporary scene was the competing ideal of the bodhisattva as a life career. In this sense we can see Buddhism as playing a significant role in challenging Song Confucians to reformulate classic values in new ways.

In this case, however, Fan's idea of the Confucian career or vocation contrasts with the bodhisattva ideal in giving priority to action in response to human needs, rather than in first seeking enlightenment and then returning to share it with other suffering humans. At the same time, the ideal of heroic, self-denying human service in the Noble Person may well owe something to the ideal of self-sacrifice in popular representations of the bodhisattva. It is an idealism which became important both to political and social reformism and to an extremely demanding conception of the Noble Person's leadership responsibility—not as a privileged aristocracy but as a moral and cultural elite. This high standard could inspire feats of heroism in later Neo-Confucians, but it could also have negative consequences when perceived as too strict and demanding a lifestyle for most men—about which more later.

Two other examples may be given of this Song Confucian response to the challenge of Buddhism. The premium which the former placed on secular learning and education, as compared to the Buddhist priority on spiritual training for emancipation from suffering, evoked new educational formulations from the Confucian side. One noteworthy formulation came from Hu Yuan (993–1059) a private teacher notable for combining classical Confucian teachings with specialization in one or another technical field of use to scholar-officials: mathematics and astronomy, hydraulic engineering (water control), law/administration, and military affairs. The classical, humanistic side of learning he categorized under three headings: substance, function, and literary expression, using classical Chinese terms also current in the exposition of Buddhist philosophy but in senses contrasting to the latter. Substance referred to classical Confucian values, function to their contemporary application, and literary expression to the importance of formulating these in terms suitable for public discourse if they were to be rendered practicable. This last concept was expressed in the term *wen*, which stood not only for written discourse but for the whole range of civil values in contrast to the military. Needless to say it contrasted with the Chan (Zen) position concerning the "inexpressibility in words" *(buli wenzi)* of Buddhist truth understood primarily as a private personal experience. Hu Yuan's formulation affirmed at once the values of civility, civil society, and civil discourse as inseparable from the Confucian Way.

This general view underlay a wide range of political, social, and economic reforms advocated or undertaken by Song Confucian leaders in the eleventh and twelfth centuries, whose political idealism and optimism was expressed in a saying attributed to the Cheng brothers: "If there is a great reform, there can be great peace and order." In the Northern Song period, however, the actual results of these reform efforts were mixed at best, and in the longer run the most lasting achievement of this movement was on the philosophical plane and in education—in defining a new leadership elite, a new educational program for that leadership (the elite, *shi* or *shidafu*) and the kind of civil instruction that would be appropriate for commoners not vouch-safed the higher education of the *shi*. All three of these purposes were to be based on a new philosophy of human nature that would deal with challenges posed by Buddhism.

What follows is a précis of this philosophy of human nature *(xing li xue)*, generally as it was summed up by Zhu Xi (1130–1200) and as it relates to the Neo-Confucian conception of the Noble Person, his education and the kind of civility to be encouraged among those who do not participate in formal schooling. The key texts prepared by Zhu Xi for use mainly in schools were *Reflections on Things at Hand (Jinsilu)* and his commentaries on the *Great Learning (Daxue)* and the *Mean (Zhongyong)* (the latter two, along with the *Analects* of Confucius and the book of Mencius, constituting Zhu Xi's Four Books). A separate anthology, the *Elementary Learning (Xiaoxue),* dealt with pre-school training.

The first chapter in *Reflections on Things at Hand,* entitled "The Substance of the Way," asserted the substantial reality of the Way in contrast to the Buddhist Way premised on the law of impermanence and the insubstantiality of all things (in the Theravada) and on the principle of Emptiness in the Mahayana (another way of expressing their insubstantiality and untenability). Zhu predicated the Supreme Ultimate *(taiji)* as the ground and first principle of the Way, intangible and ultimately illimitable, but nonetheless real, as a directive principle (like the North Star) and as an inherent genetic principle providing all things with a norm for their own growth and perfection. Zhu further asserted that all things were a compound of such an inherent, genetic principle *(li)* and of matter/energy (or life force, qi) as the basic stuff in which the principle inhered.

On this basis, Zhu also dealt with the problem of change

as a process of life and growth, rather than as one of impermanence, insubstantiality, and negation (and of the need to be delivered from the cycle of transmigratory suffering and illusion). The Confucian classic that dealt with change, the *Classic of Changes (Yijing)*, was also the textual source for the Supreme Ultimate and for understanding it as the unitary principle underlying the Way as a dynamic process of change and growth—a Way that combined genetic structure (principle) with the life force inherent in matter/energy. This view of the life force as both dynamic and directed by a normative principle accorded with the Mencian view of the self or person as a psychosomatic unity whose moral sentiments were natural expressions of human feelings. Mencius had identified these natural sentiments as the Four Seeds or Beginnings of virtue: the innate sense of empathy or commiseration, which if cultivated and directed by principle would develop into the virtue of humaneness *(ren);* the sense of shame which could be developed into the virtue of rightness or propriety *(i);* the sense of deference and respect which could be developed into the virtue of ritual decorum; and the sense of right and wrong which, when cultivated, would become wisdom.

For Mencius these four seeds, sprouts, or beginnings were common to all men and constituted the substantial nature of all human beings; they were real because they corresponded to actual human feelings and related to the conduct of life in human society—in contrast to the realization of an ineffable Buddha-nature. For Zhu Xi they were coordinate with the order of the life principle (the Supreme Ultimate) in all things, but since principle always exhibited elements of both unity and diversity, or commonality and difference, the task of cultivating virtue always had to take into account both commonality (a shared nature) and individual difference in dealing with the self, others, and the things of the world. Thus the Neo-Confucians spoke of the unity of principle and diversity of its particularizations *(li-i fen shu)*. In human beings this diversity arose from individual selves, each with its own psycho-physical nature, including appetites and desires that needed to be directed and cultivated in accordance with the moral, rational nature common to all.

To cultivate and perfect this individual nature was the common task of all human beings. The leadership elite whose education bore a special responsibility for promoting the welfare of the people might hold themselves to the higher standard of the Noble Person, but the civility on which human civilization depended, though perhaps not aiming so high, was cultivated on the basis of the same common nature. Hence Zhu Xi spoke of "self-cultivation for the governance of humankind" *(xiuji zhiren)* (that is, governance relying on universal self-discipline of both rulers and ruled), and this became widely accepted in East Asian societies as a political slogan.

Put in this form, the Neo-Confucian program was premised on a common philosophy of human nature and its cultivation, underlying both the heroic nobility expected of the leadership elite and the civility expected of all. In both cases the stress was on individual duty and responsibility, starting with self-understanding *(zide)* and self-cultivation *(xiuji)* but immediately engaging with others, at first in the family and eventually the community, the state, and humankind at large (all-under-Heaven).

While the prime focus was on humankind, it should be noted that "all-under-Heaven" included all of creation, including the natural world, for the principles inhering in human nature were related to the principles inhering in all things. Thus the full dimensions of human cultivation could only be achieved by relating the self to "all-under-Heaven." This was expressed in the ideal of the "humaneness which forms one body with Heaven-and-earth and all things" *(Tiandi wanwu yiti zhiren),* based on common affinity and the inherent capability of empathetic understanding in humankind (an affinity which might be understood in a way analogous to the magnetic or gravitational attraction among all things). In this sense the ideals of both nobility and civility opened up onto a larger horizon of global or universal commonality and the concept of public-mindedness (or what might be called "open-heartedness" or "fair-mindedness") *(gong)* was not, theoretically, limited to human affairs in the narrow sense, but extended to nature as well.

As a practical matter, the process of cultivation began for all, regardless of class or station, in the home. It was set forth by Zhu Xi in the *Elementary Learning,* citing the Confucian classics and historical examples. Starting with infant care (indeed even prenatal care), it went on to the child's learning of household chores and family duties, then how one dealt with human relations, and finally how one developed self-respect through cultivation of one's person.[2]

Two points were especially stressed: first, that there should be a definite method of instruction, staged, graduated, and ordered according to a sequential pattern of learning in a maturing person; second, that the cultivation of social relations—the Five (paradigmatic) Human Relationships—was integral to one's self-development. These were the relationships of parent/child; ruler/minister (or subordinate); husband/wife; older and younger siblings; and between friends. As personal relationships, each of these had specific moral obligations which naturally attached to them, and as dual relations they were marked by both a common bond and differentiated responsibilities toward one another. For instance, in the case of the parent/child relationship, the common bond was intimate affection, and this could be expressed as caring for one another, but the care given in each case would differ according to the needs and capabilities of each. Similarly, between ruler and minister the common bond or shared value was the obligation "to do right," but in "doing right" the superior and subordinate had their respective functions to perform. All such cases illustrated the concept of "the unity of principle and the diversity of its particularizations." (Parenthetically, note that, contrary to a wide misconception, the prime value of the parent/child relationship was not filial piety, nor in the case of ruler/minister was it loyalty.)

It is noteworthy that these paradigmatic relations were common and central both to the *Elementary Learning* (for "everyman" or every child in the home setting) and to the basic charter Zhu drew up for the White Deer Academy, which became a model for the schooling of educated youth throughout East Asia. Since education by formal schooling on a higher level entailed the prospect of public service, while *Elementary Learning* was for all, we can see again a continuity and consistency between "nobility" for the leadership elite and common "civility" in this educational philosophy and program. This is true also in the case of the classic text Zhu Xi gave priority to in his program of formal schooling: the *Great Learning*. This learning began with cultivating one's moral nature, but in accordance with the idea that one would not cultivate one's own nature apart from the moral relations just cited, Zhu's second, and almost concurrent priority was "to renew the people *(xin min)*" that is, to help others to cultivate themselves. Thus the cultivation of the Noble Person necessarily involved some responsibility for seeing to the education of all. Accordingly, in his preface to the *Great Learning,* Zhu cited universal schooling from the capital down to the village level, as the model set by the early sage-kings. In this too nobility and civility were co-implicated.

The theme of the unity and diversity of all creation was key to Zhu Xi's method of self-cultivation, just as the latter was key to human governance. In the method Zhu spelled out in his commentaries on the *Great Learning* and the *Mean,* an empathetic understanding of others and of all things was seen as essential. The method of the *Great Learning,* known as the Eight Items or Steps, consisted of (1) investigating things; (2) extending knowledge or learning; (3) making one's intentions sincere; (4) rectifying one's mind; (5) cultivating one's person; (6) regulating the family; (7) ordering the state; and (8) bringing peace to all-under-Heaven.

What Zhu Xi meant by investigating things *(gewu)* was not simply learning about them in an empirical or objective way, but entering into them in a way that overcame the subject/object dichotomy or that was informed by some value perspective—how one related to the thing known and how it related to some larger pattern or whole. In Zhu's words:

> "The extension of knowing lies in the investigation of things" means that if we wish to extend our knowing, it

consists in fathoming the principle of any thing or affair we come into contact with, for the intelligent [spiritual] human mind always has principles inherent in the capacity to know [learn], and the things and affairs of this world all have their principles to be understood, but if a principle remains un-fathomed, one's knowing [learning] is not fully utilized. Hence the initial teaching of the Great Learning insists that the learner, as he comes upon the things of this world, must proceed from principles already known and further fathom them until he reaches the limit. After exerting himself for some time, he will one day experience a breakthrough to integral comprehension. Then the qualities of all things, whether internal or external, refined or coarse, will all be apprehended and the mind, in its whole substance and great functioning, will all be clearly manifested, This is "things [having been] investigated." This is the utmost of knowing. (729)

Zhu's reference to a sudden "breakthrough to integral comprehension" carried with it a sense of self-realization and self-fulfillment akin to a holistic experience, and it is not surprising that some understood it as an enlightenment similar in certain respects but different in approach from Chan (Zen) Buddhism. Interpretation of this suggestive passage remained highly controversial among later Neo-Confucians. What seems clear is that Zhu Xi thought of this culmination neither as a comprehensive grasp of em-pirical knowledge (in the sense of encyclopedic learning, "knowing everything") nor as a trans-rational, trans-moral gnosis ("knowing nothing"), but rather as a thorough em-pathetic understanding or enlargement of the spirit that overcomes any sense of self and other, inner and outer, sub-jective and objective.

A similar view underlay another famous formula of self-cultivation in Zhu's preface to the *Mean (zhongyong)*. In its initial formulation it consisted of sixteen characters in somewhat arcane classical language, which may be rendered as "The human mind-heart is precarious; the mind of the Way is subtle; be discriminating, be unified, hold fast to the Mean." As Zhu explained it, the "precariousness of the human mind and heart" arose from their being delicately balanced between proper and improper desires. Proper desires meant what was right for oneself and fair to others; improper ones, not right for oneself or others. To be discriminating meant to distinguish between the two, and to be unified meant to overcome any difference between one's self and others' desires or interests. For present purposes it is important to note that "oneness" or "being unified" meant understanding and acting in a way that was fair, open-minded, and served the general or public interest.

The context of this sixteen-word formula is one of governance according to the large-minded, public-spirited rule of the early sage-kings. Thus Zhu began his preface to the *Mean* as follows:

> Why was the *Mean* written? Master Zisi wrote it because he was worried lest the transmission of the Learning of the Way *(daoxue)* be lost. When the divine sages of highest antiquity had succeeded to the work of Heaven and established the Supreme Norm [of governance], the transmission of the Succession to the Way *(daotong)* had its inception. As may be discovered from the classics, "hold fast the Mean" [*Analects* 20:1] is what Shun transmitted to Yu.[3] Yao's one utterance is complete and perfect in itself, but Shun added three more in order to show that Yao's one utterance could only be carried out in this way. . . .

As I have maintained, the mind in its empty spirituality [pure intelligence and consciousness] is one and only one. But if we make a distinction between the human mind and the mind of the Way, it is because consciousness differs insofar as it may spring from the self-centeredness of one's individual physical form or may have its source in the correctness of one's innate nature and moral imperative. This being so, the one [human mind] may be precarious and insecure, while the other [mind of the Way] may be subtle and barely perceptible. But humans all have physical form, so even the wisest do not lack this human mind [of conflicted desires]; and all have the inborn moral nature, so even the most stupid do not lack the mind of the Way.

These two [tendencies] are mixed together in the square-inch of the mind-and-heart, and if one does not know how to order them, the precariousness becomes even more precarious, and the barely perceptible becomes even less perceptible, so that the sense of the common good [impartiality] of Heaven's principle [in the mind of the Way] is unable in the end to overcome the selfishness of human desires. "Be discriminating" means to distinguish between the two and not let them be confused. "Be unified [with the mind of the Way]" means to preserve the correctness of the original mind and not become separated from it. If one applies oneself to this without any interruption, making sure that the mind of the Way is master of one's self and that the human mind always listens to its commands, then the precariousness and insecurity will yield to peace and security, and what is subtle and barely perceptible will become clearly manifest. Then, whether in action or repose, in whatever one says or does, one will not err by going too far or not far enough.

Yao, Shun, and Yu were great sages among all-under-Heaven, and for them to pass on succession to [rulership of] the world was a major matter for all-under-Heaven. As great sages performing a major undertaking for all-under-Heaven, on such momentous occasions their repeated admonitions still consisted only of these few words. How then could anything more be added to this from among all the principles under Heaven?[4]

At least two things are worth noting in the foregoing passage. First, this formula was allegedly enunciated by the early sage-kings as the key to governance but it took the form of a maxim for all, rulers and ruled alike. Second, its political and social context, as well as its moral tone, reflect the primacy of human concerns, especially the unity (harmony) of the individual with the larger human and natural whole. As a method of self-cultivation emphasizing "discrimination" (meaning moral and rational judgment in regard to what was fair and proper to advance vis-à-vis the balance [the *Mean*] of private and public interests), it contrasted sharply with the idea of "non-discrimination" in the Mahayana Buddhist philosophy of Non-duality. Hence, in the case cited earlier of Tokugawa Ieyasu meeting with Hayashi Razan, the latter felt obliged to take issue with Ieyasu's Non-dualistic conception of the *Mean*.

In the subsequent spread and development of Neo-Confucianism, the Five Human Relations, Eight Items or Steps of the *Great Learning,* and the Sixteen-Word formula for the direction of the mind-and-heart were at the core of teaching and learning. As concise pivotal concepts, they were naturally subject to interpretation, and controversy was only heightened by the terse, cryptic, and sometimes obscure language in which they were expressed. This was especially true of the concept of unity or oneness, which, like the Way itself, was open-ended and ultimately undefinable. But the essential method seems clear enough—for both the Noble Person and the commoner, it was to do what was right and fair in the larger human interest and in the perspective of all-under-Heaven.

If, however, the basic principle of Zhu Xi put the primary responsibility for social order on the individual, this left a great deal open as to how or in what form the individual's efforts and needs would be mediated to society as a whole. Zhu himself was not unaware of this problem or of the practical difficulties in the way of implementing his program. As an official, his days at court were limited (as both a renowned scholar and gadfly it was an awkward fit for both him and the ruler), and so he found himself more often assigned to local or provincial posts, where he tried to address problems on that level. For him, two of the most important of these were local schools and community organization.

Zhu was well aware of the difficulties encountered earlier in the Song era in trying to fulfill the ideal of universal schooling. Indeed, these proved to be chronic difficulties, unsolved even in later times, but Zhu tried to make up for this by promoting civil morality in two forms suited to the local scene. One was the posting of simple moral instructions in the form of public proclamations. Following are excerpts from a proclamation issued by Zhu at Zhang-zhou in 1190. It is important to note that although the proclamation as a whole makes some reference to functional differentiation in people's duties, the main contents are addressed to "gentlemen *(shi)* [that is, leaders in the community], and commoners" alike. In other words, Zhu is addressing the need for a common public morality in the community as a whole:

1. Instructions to members of community units *(baowu)* on matters about which they should encourage and remind each other: All members should encourage and remind each other to be filial to parents, respectful to elders, cordial to clansmen and relatives, and helpful to neighbors. Each should perform his assigned duty and engage in his primary occupation. None should commit vicious acts or thefts, or indulge in drinking or gambling. They should not fight with or sue each other. . . .

3. Instructions to gentlemen *(shi)* and commoners *(min):* People should understand that our body originates from our parents and that brothers come from the same source. Thus, we are endowed by nature with a feeling of obligation to parents and brothers, most profound and grave. What makes us love our parents or respect our elder brothers is not forced but comes spontaneously from the original mind-and-heart. And this love is inexhaustible. . . .

5. Instructions to gentlemen and commoners: People should be kind and cordial toward villagers, neighbors, clansmen, and relatives. If sometimes a minor quarrel occurs, both parties should reflect deeply and make every effort to negotiate and reach a reconciliation. They should not lightly bring lawsuits. Even if one is right, one's property will become diminished and one's work and livelihood may be cut off. How much worse is it if one is not right? In that case one cannot avoid imprisonment and punishment. (749–750)

To promote a sense of community Zhu also recommended community granaries and social rituals that would bring people together in a cooperative spirit. The most important of these was the community compact, which brought villagers together periodically for mutual encouragement and assistance. As a whole, the compact meetings in the form recommended by Zhu expressed his conviction that education through joint participation in proper rites and community functions is more effective for achieving social harmony and promoting the general welfare than attempts at forced indoctrination or punitive law. Zhu's recommendations fell under four main headings: (1) mutual encouragement of virtue and meritorious deeds; (2) mutual correction of faults; (3) mutual association in rites and customs; and (4) mutual sympathy [aid] in calamities and difficulties. Other provisions specify the leadership, organization, and conduct of meetings of the members, described in precise detail but too extensive to be reported on here.

The opening lines of the text may suffice to convey the general tone of the public morality or civility Zhu tried to promote.

> "Virtue" means being sure to act upon seeing the good and being sure to reform upon hearing of faults; to be able to govern oneself; to be able to govern one's family; to be able to serve father and elder brothers; to be able to instruct sons and younger brothers; to be able to manage servants; to be able to serve superiors; to be friendly with relatives and acquaintances; to be able to choose friends; to be able to maintain integrity; to be able to extend kindness; to be able to plan things for people; to be able to accomplish things for the people; to be able to resolve conflicts; to be able to decide right and wrong; to be able to promote the beneficial and abolish the harmful; to be able to hold offices and reinvigorate offices.
>
> "Meritorious deeds" means, at home, serving one's father and elder brothers, instructing one's children and younger brothers, and managing one's wife and concu-

bines. Outside, it means serving one's superiors, entertaining friends, instructing students, and managing servants. As to reading books, overseeing the fields, managing the household, helping creatures, and favoring the practice of rites, music, archery, charioteering, writing, and arithmetic—all are the kinds of things that should be done. To do anything not of that kind is of no benefit.

The foregoing virtuous deeds should be the subjects of individual emulation and mutual encouragement. At meetings of the compact members they should be cited as cause for mutual congratulation, and the names of those performing them should be recorded for the encouragement or admonition of others. (752)

As one can see, the basic ethical conduct of the community compact and of Zhu Xi's proclamation is much the same, and this is what became the core of popular education (outside of formal schooling) in China, Japan, and Korea, though often it was subject to adaptation and modification by other factors at work in different societies which strongly conditioned the outcome.

LATER OUTCOMES

The spread of Zhu Xi's philosophy and educational program throughout East Asia is attributable to the efforts initially of scholars through local, semiprivate academies; only later did these scholars persuade rulers to adopt them officially—but with mixed results.

The Mongol ruler Khubilai was the first to authorize the adoption of Zhu Xi's curriculum in the Imperial Academy and state schools, but his authorization to establish a universal school system, as recommended to him by an exponent of Zhu's teaching, was never seriously implemented. Later in 1313–1315, still under the Mongols, Zhu's curriculum, based primarily on the Four Books, was incorporated in the civil service examination system and remained there under successive dynasties, with all the advantages and drawbacks attaching thereto. Since most students with access to schooling aimed at joining the official ranks, in school they generally followed the examination curriculum, and in the process became exposed to Zhu Xi's educational philosophy, which itself went beyond the official uses of his texts for examination purposes. From this a constant tension arose between Zhu Xi's "learning for one's self" and learning for worldly success in officialdom.

The "learning for sagehood" built into this philosophy in the Song was linked to but not wholly encompassed by our concepts of Nobility and Civility; this was the ideal of the self or individual as called to achieve the spiritual perfection of sagehood. Undoubtedly, this aim reflected another of the subtle challenges of Buddhism, which in spreading (and indeed popularizing) the universality of the Buddha nature, had prompted Neo-Confucians to expand, as well as deepen, their own concept of sagehood and the universality of principle in the form of the human moral nature. Simply put, the Confucian sage was to be thought of not just as an early sage-king, a model for rulers, but as an ideal of spiritual perfection corresponding to the Supreme Ultimate in each individual. But inevitably (a word I use advisedly) the positing of such a high ideal meant installing— indeed intruding—an element that would stand in sharp contrast to the existing state of affairs and create much ferment within Neo-Confucianism.

The new spirituality of the Neo-Confucian sage (typified

by the equanimity and indeed joy attributed to one of Confucius' disciples, Yan Hui, even though he lived in poverty and humble station) gave a further lofty dimension to the heroic stature of the Noble Person. While the latter had been asked by Fan Zhongyan to put the world's worries ahead of his own pleasures, the ideal of the sage offered the prospect of an integral wholeness and spiritual serenity that transcended both worry and pleasure. In the Ming period there are many cases of Confucian ministers standing up to despotic emperors and suffering martyrdom with this kind of equanimity.

Beyond these cases of heroic Confucian scholars, there is the special case of the Empress Hsü, consort of one of these Ming despots, who insisted that, as all human beings possess the moral/rational nature, all are called to achieve the perfection of sagehood, women as well as men. This justified her following her mentor the Empress Ma (consort of the Ming founder), in playing a strong role at court as Mother of the People, and not leaving everything to her husband or always yielding to him (831).

In the Ming era many dedicated Neo-Confucians chose not to compromise themselves by taking office under a corrupt and despotic dynasty, but rather sought independently to pursue the cultivation of spirituality and integrity. Among these the most striking, as well as the most celebrated, is Wang Yangming, whose career went from youthful nonconformism to a brilliant (but nonetheless tragic) career as statesman, general, and teacher. Briefly put, Wang reconceived the task of achieving sage status in the midst of official involvement (or indeed in any real-life situation) by affirming that self-cultivation should start, not from scholarly or intellectual pursuits, but from the natural expression of one's moral nature, extending one's innate knowledge outward from one's innermost self to engagement with the world. To put it another way, instead of working to achieve knowledge and arrive at some mature sense or state of unity with Heaven-and-earth and all things, one should act on and express the innate sentiments of one's original moral nature as already integral with Heaven-and-earth. This latter method did not depend so much on the acquisition of learning or scholarly achievement as on the activation of one's natural moral sensibilities as a guide to one's learning experience.

To express Sagely Learning in these simple terms as a direct response to life situations was to expand considerably the accessibility of the ideal sage to anyone and everyone—without regard to qualifications of learning or official accreditation. As the saying went, "the streets are full of sages." And as Wang's teachings spread, they inspired many popular social, literary, and educational movements. Among these, of particular relevance to our theme here is his interest in resurrecting the idea of community compacts as a way of stimulating public morality and civil association. For the most part, Wang's version of the compact remained faithful to Zhu Xi's, but he saw it as meeting a particular need of his own time—the peaceful reintegration of people who had become disaffected with the established order. At that time, in sixteenth-century Ming China, many scholars and conscientious officials shared the same concern and became active in the same cause. One reason for this was the breakdown of the system of local administration established by the founder of the Ming dynasty. Although the workings of that system and its failings are not our concern here, the early enactments of the Ming founder help to explain what had happened to the idea of the community compact and why sixteenth-century reformers like Wang Yangming had tried to resurrect it.

CIVILITY, IMPERIAL STYLE

The founder of the Ming dynasty, Chu Yuanzhang (r. 1368–1398), rose from the ranks of commoners to dominate a chaotic military scene and reunify China after a prolonged period of civil strife at the end of Mongol rule. As a self-made, self-educated peasant, he was proud of his success in imposing order on an anarchic situation—the legacy of lax, incompetent Mongol rule. As he put it:

> When I was young I was orphaned and poor and grew up amidst warfare. At the age of twenty-four I joined the ranks and was ordered about for three years. Then I gathered together able followers and studied the ways of training soldiers, planning to compete with the warlords. It was trying and worrisome. I was apprehensive and on guard for nearly twenty years until I was able to eliminate powerful enemies and unite the empire. Of human deceit I have known plenty. Therefore, drawing on what I have seen and done, together with the officials I have fixed the law of the land. This has eliminated the indulgent rule of the Yuan dynasty and those who defiled the old customs. The warlords were powerful and deceitful. They were hard to govern, but I have governed them. The people, encountering disorder, tried by all manner of evil means to pass through the unrest. They were hard to manage, but I have managed them (781)

As a commoner, Chu was also something of a populist and early on was inclined to adopt systems like Zhu Xi's community schools and community compacts. But when he ran into difficulties with establishing local schools, he quickly backed off and allowed, in effect, the privatization of local schooling by leaving it to local families able to manage it themselves. The community compact he folded in with Zhu Xi's proclamation to the people on the essentials of civil conduct or public morality. His "Placard for the Instruction of the People" included the following provision:

> In each village and *li* [local grouping] a bell with a wooden clapper shall be prepared. Old persons, disabled persons unable to function normally, or blind persons shall be selected and guided by children to walk through the *li* holding the bell. If there are no such persons in the *li*, then they shall be selected from other *li*. Let them shout loudly so that everyone can hear, urging people to do good and not violate the law. Their message is: "Be filial to your parents, respect elders and superiors, live in harmony with neighbors, instruct and discipline children and grandchildren, be content with your occupation, commit no wrongful acts." (790)

From this provision developed what was literally called the Community Compact (*xiangyue*) meeting, no doubt because the moral maxims that constituted the core of the proclamation were still recognized as coming from Zhu Xi's earlier Proclamation and Community Compact. In later years this practice, bearing the prestige of the founding father of the dynasty, developed into a periodic public meeting at which the magistrate or his surrogate lectured on public morality, to the accompaniment of popular entertainment in the vernacular dramatizing the moral lessons to be conveyed. Only a few scholars were conscious of its derivation from Zhu Xi or, like Wang Yangming, were mindful of its original purpose. Its authority thus became more associated with the Emperor than with Zhu.

This standard practice of the Ming was continued by the (Manchu) Qing dynasty, with an increasingly authoritarian tone and content, emphasizing loyalty to the throne and obedience to the authorities. The standard Qing vision became definitive in the reign of the Yongzheng emperor (r. 1723–1735), who added ten more precepts to Zhu Xi's original Six. These were of an authoritarian and bureaucratic character that was quite foreign to the spirit of Zhu Xi's original community compact—they pertained to law as administered by the territorial agents of state administration; to collective security units; to the ostracizing of deserters and miscreants; to the prompt payment of taxes; to the suppression of heterodoxy—none of which were mentioned by Zhu Xi. Also striking here is the attention to scholarly achievement, which the accompanying commentary and popular expositions clearly connect with advancement through the examination system, the prime means of official recruitment. Ironically, Zhu Xi, the great scholar himself, had said nothing whatever about scholarly training in his village compact; here, however, it ranks well ahead of Zhu's instructions to the young in general, which had been oriented toward moral conduct in the family, neighborhood, and village community, not to success in the state bureaucracy.

So widespread was this official practice in the Ming and Qing periods that it early came to the attention of foreign observers, who noted its official character, its emphasis on compliance with the authorities, and the fact that it had tended to become a ritual routine, dutifully performed by mandarins as an official function but not taken too seriously by anyone.

In contrast to the routinization of this custom, also known as the Village Lectures, the Ming founder's "sage instructions" became increasingly thought of as a Sacred Edict, reflecting the theocratic character of the monarchy and the process of official ritualization by which the performance became endowed with a quasi-religious aura.

Again, few contemporaries realized the extent to which this was a transformation of Zhu Xi's original Community Compact, which had promoted such communitarian values as the leadership responsibility of the local elite, consensual agreement among the members at village meetings (the "compact"), popular moral uplift, neighborly cooperation, and mutual aid, with ceremonial respect shown for age and superior wisdom but otherwise no distinctions made of rank or class. This original character is still reflected in the preservation of Zhu Xi's Six Precepts among the later Sixteen. Moreover, despite the aggrandizing of imperial authority in the official Ming and Qing versions, priority is still given to the family values of filiality and brotherliness (especially as dramatized in later popular tales of heroic filial piety), while the virtue of loyalty to the throne (not mentioned in Zhu Xi's version, or even in the early Ming version, out of respect for Zhu's original formulation) is again striking for its absence from this otherwise markedly theocratic ritual.

When the nineteenth-century British scholar, James Legge, noted the importance of the Village Lectures and the Sacred Edict ("Sacred" here meaning "Imperial"), he characterized it as Imperial Confucianism. Yet while the long-term trend through the Ming and Qing was for Zhu Xi's precepts to be appropriated in this authoritarian and bureaucratic way for the purposes of the state, conscientious Confucian scholars and officials like Wang Yangming, aware of this diversion from Zhu's original aim, wanted to retrieve Zhu Xi's communitarian ideal and implement it as a voluntaristic, cooperative organization with some degree of local autonomy.

For a variety of reasons, including the early success of the Manchus in reestablishing a strong centralized, bureaucratic state, the efforts of these reformers did not succeed. The irony of this communitarianism's failure in China may be appreciated when seen in contrast to the success of Neo-Confucians in Korea, including leading thinkers and scholars committed to Zhu Xi's philosophy, in establishing the community compact as a form of local organization and civil practice. Though highly relevant to any consideration of the transnational, universalistic character of Zhu Xi's conception of civil morality, for a fuller account of this development one may have recourse to other published works.[5]

7

Civil and Military in Tokugawa Japan

In Japan, even with the wide spread of Neo-Confucianism in the Tokugawa period, the community compact had much less success as an organization than in Korea—a failure that has been explained as owing to an entrenched system of local organization and strong, hierarchical feudal relations in Japan.[1] Nevertheless the Six Precepts had a history of their own, quite relevant to the problem of how Zhu Xi's concepts of civil morality fared in different systemic contexts in East Asia. The story starts, however, with what may seem to be a historical accident.

In the East Asian maritime trade of the sixteenth and seventeenth centuries it was not unusual for books to circulate on the sea lanes among China, Korea, Japan, the Ryūkyūs, Taiwan, Vietnam, and on into Southeast Asia. But word concerning the Six Precepts reached Japan in the form of a vernacular commentary on the Six Precepts (*Liu yü yan yi*) by a late Ming scholar, Fan Hong, and came by a somewhat circuitous and unlikely route, having been forwarded through the King of the Ryūkyūs to the Lord of

Satsuma and thence to Shogun Tokugawa Yoshimune (r. 1716–1745). The latter had Ogyū Sorai (1666–1728) punctuate Fan's text in Japanese style, and had Muro Kyūsō (1658–1734) translate it into the Japanese vernacular, which he did with the assistance of a professional translator from Nagasaki, more expert than Muro Kyūsō in the Ming vernacular.

Muro's *The General Sense of the Extended Meaning of the Six Precepts (Rikuyu engi taigi)* was not simply a translation of Fan Hong's work, but rather a digest in the same genre as Xu Heng's digest of Zhu Xi's *Elementary Learning (Xiaoxue dayi)* and other works of Zhu Xi's summarized by Xu in vernacular form for the Mongol emperor Khubilai. Fan's *Extended Meaning,* by contrast, had expanded on the Six Precepts in the same way as Zhen Dexiu (1178–1235) had done in his *Extended Meaning of the Great Learning (Daxue yanyi).*[2] Thus popularization underwent successive phases of expansion, contraction, encapsulization, and translation.

Muro Kyūsō was not only a strong adherent of Zhu Xi but a notable advocate of Zhu's ideal of universal schooling—for women as well as men. In this light the *General Sense* may be seen as a fair and sympathetic representation of Zhu's overall intent. In contrast, the other scholar, Sorai, was critical of Zhu Xi, had doubts about the wisdom of raising people's political consciousness through popular education, and opposed the dissemination of the *Extended Meaning of the Six Precepts.*

Subsequently the Shogun Yoshimune authorized the promulgation of Muro's *General Sense of the Extended Meaning of the Six Precepts* not only to his own domains but to outer ones as well. Over forty versions were in print and still extant in the late nineteenth century. Indeed, this text became a prime source for the celebrated Imperial Rescript on Education of the Emperor Meiji, though only a few scholars in recent times have been aware of its origins or the successive adaptations the *Six Precepts* had undergone.

In the Meiji version there is a strong emphasis on loyalty to the Emperor, serving the purposes of the new nation-state, but this is lacking in Zhu Xi's original, which emphasized filial piety as the common human ground of public morality and said nothing about loyalty to the ruler. Muro's version is faithful to Zhu Xi. If he had wished to promote loyalty to the ruler, he might have done so in his vernacular exposition of the second maxim. Instead he kept to Zhu Xi's original concept of family and communitarian roles, not loyalty to state or emperor. In a post-face to his *General Significance,* Muro states:

The [Confucian classic] *Rites of Zhou* speaks of people meeting for the reading of the laws, and later worthies [esp. Zhu Xi] spoke of community compact meetings. These were to supplement education in the schools so as to support and sustain public morality. . . . But after the school system ceased to be maintained [as provided in the *Rites* and advocated by Zhu Xi], the people received instruction only by government edict, so the ruler had to worry about how effectively his efforts at edification reached down into the village. Laws proliferated, punishments increased, regulations multiplied and enforcement became more strictly detailed [to no avail]. . . . Then in the Ming there was a plethora of imperial admonitions and edicts, of laws and regulations promulgated throughout the land, which were followed up by the Six Precepts of the Qing Emperor [Kang

Xi] for the regulation of his conquered empire and emulation by his subjects. But how could this be done with barbarians imposing on the civilized Chinese? As it happened, however, Fan Hong of Huiji had [already] written his *Extended Meaning of the Six Precepts* in vernacular Chinese, which served the educational purpose well."

Muro then goes on to explain that his work in Japanese may serve the same purpose for Japan, which claims to be a "land of Confucian noble men." He faithfully lists the Six Precepts as:

1. Be filial and obedient to your parents
2. Respect your seniors and superiors
3. Harmonize and cooperate with your community
4. Instruct your children and grandchildren
5. Be content with your own livelihood
6. Do nothing one shouldn't do.[3]

Muro's vernacular Japanese commentary stays close to Fan Hong's version, which itself keeps to the original Six Precepts without the more legalistic and bureaucratic additions of the Qing. As such, Muro's interpretation reflects the original emphasis of Zhu Xi on filiality as the basis of public morality. Had he been inclined to substitute loyalty to the ruler for filial piety, the natural place to have done so would have been in his interpretation of the second maxim, respect for seniors and superiors, extending it upward to include those on high. Muro did not do this however; he kept rather to Zhu Xi's basic family and communitarian model, rather than go along with the Qing adaptation of the Instructions to serve the purposes of the ruler and his state—nor, it may be added, did he go along with other Edo period thinkers who, writing for samurai and not commoners, put the virtue of loyalty ahead of filial piety.

The wide spread of the Six Precepts in this form is evidenced not only by their promulgation by local officials, but also, indirectly, by their appearing in the House Code of the Okaya House (1836)[4] as the basis for the lectures of Hosoi Heishū (1728–1801), an extremely popular free-lance teacher in late eighteenth-century Japan. This influence is further reflected in their incorporation into the famous Imperial Rescript on Education of the Emperor Meiji (1890). As so often happened when appropriated for Imperial purposes, the Six Precepts were then put to very different uses from what Zhu Xi intended, but even this misappropriation evidences a desire to exploit the wide currency these values had achieved among an increasingly literate Japanese population in the late eighteenth, early nineteenth century.

Before proceeding to that next stage in Japanese history, we will do well to consider one other example of the civility promoted by Neo-Confucianism. Thus far we have dealt with it primarily on the level of the village community, and this is certainly appropriate for an East Asia still predominantly agricultural and for societies still operating mostly at the opposing poles of local village and central state.

But in the sixteenth and seventeenth centuries a maritime trade was growing along the East Asian littoral (as seen in the circuitous sea route taken by the Six Precepts). This activity was peripheral to China and Korea, and not a major concern of their rulers, with their attention necessarily focused on more immediate domestic matters. Somewhat differently, however, the feudal rulers of Japan (including Tokugawa Ieyasu) and merchants who participated in the maritime trade were engaged in intercoastal enterprises, which also involved them in intercultural negotiations and communication.

The following case illustrates how one such negotiation

was carried on between the Japanese and Vietnamese (at that time the state of Annam), with Ieyasu an interested party, advised by Fujiwara Seika (1561–1619), the teacher of the aforementioned Hayashi Razan. Seika was trying diplomatically to mend relations strained by the misbehavior of Japanese merchantmen party to this coastal trade, and he argues his case on much the same grounds Razan did when explaining to Ieyasu his concept of legitimacy of rulers as based on their proper behavior—to be judged by how one resolves questions of fairness in distinguishing between competing interests of the shared or common good and private or self-interest.

In a letter addressed to the ruler of Annam, Seika assumes that the latter shares the same Neo-Confucian culture as other East Asians influenced by the latest civilizational trends from China. This includes a familiarity with Zhu Xi's Four Books, especially the *Great Learning,* and with the Five Constant Human Relations as the basis of one's understanding of the human moral nature. In some contrast to the four values centered on family relations and superior/subordinate relations, here Seika generalizes from the one relation which is based on parity, mutual trust, and reciprocity—the relationship among friends. Fair trade (not just "free trade" ungoverned by normative principles) is the issue. But it is also trade conducted under the aegis of the local ruler, so Seika has to explain trust as a value common to both rulers and merchants:

In your letter you quote from the *Great Learning,* and say that it is all a matter of "abiding in trustworthiness," and this one word truly expresses the essence of governing one's house and teaching the country. Trust is an inherent part of our human nature. It moves heaven and earth, penetrates metal and stone, and pervades everywhere. How could its value be limited only to diplomatic relations and trade between neighboring countries? Is not this nature the reason why all men everywhere are the same, even though customs may differ when we travel a thousand leagues? If we look at things from this perspective, what is different are secondary things such as clothing and language. However, even at a distance of one thousand or ten thousand leagues, and even though clothes and speech may differ, there exists some thing that is not far off, approximately the same, that hardly differs. This is, I think, trust, which is one and universal.

My earlier emissaries behaved badly. As they traveled to and fro between your country and Japan, their actions belied their words, and often they mistook the situation. Therefore I have punished them according to the law of the land. I assume that in your country you would do the same? As a rule, the complement of a ship is recruited from among the lads of the market and shop assistants, and when they see even the slightest chance of gain, they forget the shame of the death penalty. They talk too much and in their joy or anger say whatever comes to their mouths; hence, they cannot be trusted. From now on, reliable communications between our two countries will take the form of letters, and the reliability of these letters will be established by their seals. These seals will prove that they are genuine. Therefore I have given the present crew your answering letter of this summer. Please examine it carefully. I also send you a few of our local products, as complimentary presents.

Seika next goes on to argue the case for a common humanity, not only among Japanese and Annamese but among the four classes of society as classically defined—including merchants:

> In your letter, you say that "our country is a country of poetry and history, of rites and rightness, and not a place of market-goods and traders' congregations." Indeed, when one has to do with market-goods and trade, if one only works for gain and profit, it is really despicable. However, if one discusses this in more general terms, are not all of the four classes part of the people, even the despicable merchants? Are not all of the eight responsibilities of the state of equal necessity, even trade? Outside the scope of giving peace to the people and governing them, poetry, history, rites and rightness make no sense, and without poetry, history, rites and rightness, it is impossible to give peace to the people or to govern. This is also the fixed, inherent Nature of the five quarters—the Nature which has trust as one of its principal constituents. What your country is warning against is simply that we might lose this trust, which may bring various unfortunate results. As long, however, as our two countries have not lost this trust, one single small-minded individual should not be able to cause such unfortunate results to arise. But of course, we should be on our guard. In case such an incident should arise, both countries have their codes of punishment.

Seika then proceeds to formulate a code of conduct, a compact to which all those aboard ship engaged in this trade should subscribe. For brevity's sake, just two of its clauses are cited here:

> 2. As compared to our country, other countries may differ in customs and speech, but the heavenly-endowed principle [the moral nature] has always been the same. Do not forget what is common, do not be suspicious of what is strange,

and do not ever lie or brag. Even if foreigners would not be aware of it, we should be. "Trust reaches even to pigs and fish, and trickery shows itself even to the seagulls." Heaven does not tolerate deception; you should not disgrace the manners of our country. If you meet a humane person or a noble person (*junzi*) in that country, respect him as you would your father or your teacher. Inquire into the prohibitions and taboos of that country, and adapt to its customs.

3. Between heaven that covers and earth that bears us up, all peoples are brothers and all things and affairs are shared in common, and all should be seen as one in their right to humane treatment. How much more does this apply to people from the same country? To people of the same ship? If there is trouble, sickness, cold or hunger, then all should be helped equally; do not even think of wanting to escape alone.[5]

This oath or compact invokes the same values of commonality, parity, mutual assistance, and shared benefit, as in the community compact (*xiangyue*); the same Chinese term *yue* (Japanese *yaku*) appears here in the word for oath or compact (*kiyaku*). These are also values shared by Japanese scholars and teachers from among the merchant class or townspeople (*chōnin*) who adopted and adapted the Neo-Confucian ethic to their own situation in the seventeenth and eighteenth centuries. We are warranted then in assuming it to be a popular morality widely enough shared among the Japanese people so that leaders in the late nineteenth century would want to build on it as providing some common ground for their new nationalistic ethos.

On this level of popular morality—civility codified on the level of the common people—one could say that there was significant common ground among the peoples of East Asia

influenced by Neo-Confucian culture. What remains to be
seen in the Japanese case, however, is the outcome with regard to the ideal of the Confucian Noble Man as understood on the level of the educated leadership elite.

THE CONFUCIAN NOBLE MAN AS SAMURAI

When Zhu Xi spoke about the relationship of ruler and
minister as the second of the five cardinal human relations,
he had in mind the duty of both to serve the public interest—to do what was right on behalf of common humanity
or in advancing the common good. For him this meant the
minister or official's fidelity to principle in serving as mentor to the ruler in public matters. How then would this
translate into the feudal relationships prevalent in Tokugawa Japan? The answer: it would be an awkward fit at
best.

First of all, the Japanese equivalent for the Chinese term
"ruler/minister" was generally understood as lord and vassal, lord and retainer, or lord and samurai, terms which carried with them all the medieval baggage of supposedly
undying personal loyalty of the vassal to the lord. Put another way, it meant a readiness to sacrifice everything—and
needless to say, one's life—for one's lord. The idea of advis-
ing the ruler on issues of public policy was hardly possible,
since the whole notion of "public" had become so privatized and personalized for so long. It would take some time
for Japan to become "civilized" in the Confucian or Neo-
Confucian sense, so that a predominantly civil orientation
could overtake the sense of the samurai as primarily warriors; indeed, Confucian civility came slowly to many members of the hereditary military aristocracy who were reluc-

tant to renounce the use of force or who insisted on a strict hierarchy in political consultation.

This basic fact of Japanese life was noted by one of the early proponents of Neo-Confucian ethical teaching in the seventeenth century, Nakae Tōju (1608–1648), who saw the inescapable tensions between a Way of the Warrior that celebrated spontaneous bravery and physical prowess as opposed to the rational moral judgment that should guide the leader in an age of peace and civility. In the following passage we recognize Tōju's characterization of the type of warrior seen already in the time of Nobunaga and Hideyoshi, and the alternative of restrained deliberation Neo-Confucians spoke of as the Learning of the Mind-and-Heart (*shingaku*).

A person who is born with a stout spirit and a natural talent for military prowess can master the military arts and achieve merit in battle even without training himself in the Learning of the Mind. But because he will be lacking in virtue, he will get intoxicated with his physical prowess and find killing people enjoyable. He will thus act unrighteously and unjustly, causing much suffering and lamentation among the populace. In the end he will inevitably meet with Heaven's punishment, at the cost of his own life and the destruction of his domain. . . . One only has to look at the history books of both China and Japan. The original purpose of the military arts is to assure the peace and tranquility of the state, preserve the good fortune of the warrior class, and bring the blessings of peace to the populace. If instead they become the cause of the misery of the populace, the loss of warrior lives, and the destruction of the state, then the mastery of military arts and the achievement of military merit are nothing but useless vanity. What is more, if a person knows only of intrigues, trickery, and violence and nothing of the virtues of humaneness and rightness, then even if he has the prowess of a Han Xin or Xiang Yu,[6] he will not be able to hold his shield against an enemy who has self-control. . . . If one really wants to study military arts, then why not study the military arts of the man of humaneness against which no man under heaven can stand up?

In a battle situation or at a time when the application of martial prowess is required, those involved must act valiantly. However, this is something which is useless in ordinary times of peace. In times of peace, to devote oneself constantly to acts of valor and bravery on the grounds that one is preparing oneself for battle is an ignorant pursuit, and it will not be of any use in times of emergency. . . . Those who are fond of proving their fearlessness by unprovoked acts of violence will inevitably end up treating other people with contempt and come to love conflict for its own sake, getting into fights (kenka) that end in nothing more than a meaningless death. They will cause anxiety to their parents and steal the fiefs of their lords. Even if they manage to perform "heroic deeds" in the defense of their honor, they are no different from a dog that has a strong bite. A samurai who has a heart should be ashamed of such things.[7]

As an exponent of civil virtue in contrast to military, Nakae Tōju was also known for the high priority he gave to filial piety ahead of loyalty to one's lord. Since filiality was also the prime value and shared basis of Zhu Xi's community compact, we can see how filial virtue could serve as the common ground for civility in both Neo-Confucian scholarship and the local community, as compared to loyalty among the samurai.

The contrary inclination to give feudal values priority over civil ones, lamented by the Neo-Confucian Nakae Tōju, is shown by the frequency with which the priority of parent/child and ruler/minister was reversed in the rendering of the Five Moral Relations by Japanese writers. The latter generally put ruler/minister (understood as "lord/vassal") ahead of parent/child, and loyalty to the lord ahead of filial piety as the prime virtue. Not only did this occur in formal instruction and standard texts, but it was even dramatized in such a popular Kabuki play as Chikamatsu's *Battle of Coxinga* (1715).

This play has to do with the purported rescue of a Chinese dynasty from invading Tartars, aided by a treacherous Chinese minister who assassinates his own emperor. The rescue is accomplished by the half-Japanese, half-Chinese hero Coxinga with the help of a Chinese minister, who demonstrates his loyalty by deliberately sacrificing his own infant son to save the life of the newborn heir to the Chinese throne. Although Chikamatsu makes a great show of celebrating shared Chinese and Japanese values, it is the indomitable martial spirit of the Japanese and their loyalty to the ruler (as in the case of the loyal minister sacrificing his own son and later offering to sacrifice his wife) that override all other values, including the primary Confucian relation of love between parent and child. Finally, after Coxinga and his heroic band have defeated the villainous Chinese minister, they are eulogized by Chikamatsu in the following terms:

Standing on three sides of [the traitor] Ri Tōten, they raise their swords with a great shout and in one stroke [together] they cut off his head and arms. They wish the new [Chinese] emperor Eiryaku a reign of ten thousand years [Banzai!] and offer prayers for the peace and safety of the country. This joy they owe to the divine, the martial and the saintly virtues of the Emperor of Great Japan, a land endowed with these perpetual blessings, which will prosper forever as her people prosper.[8]

Incidentally, if one wonders how the Japanese in the mid-twentieth century could have thought of themselves as saviors of East Asia, and at the turn of the millennium still think of their earlier mission as misunderstood by the Chinese, Koreans, and the rest of the world, Chikamatsu's *Coxinga* is something to consider: the Confucian "minister" as the bold samurai saving China!

An actual historical event of about the same time further illustrates how the perception of Confucian values was refracted by surviving feudal attitudes. It is the Akō Vendetta, celebrated in one of the most popular plays of the Tokugawa period, *The Treasury of Loyal Retainers (Chūshingura)*, which has to do with the vendetta of forty-seven samurai to avenge an insult to their lord and his wrongful death. (The samurai are usually referred to here as *rōnin*, masterless samurai, because the death of their lord left them without a master.) The alleged insult to their lord had come from a master of ceremonies (ritual) at the shogunal court, whose assassination by the forty-seven *rōnin* avenged the insult but provoked their condemnation by the shogunate, which ordered them to commit ritual suicide. This in turn evoked a wave of popular sympathy for these loyal samurai who had given their lives for their lord. It also evoked a wave of controversy among writers who debated the merits of the shogunate's case, as well as the *rōnins'* sense of duty and spectacular self-sacrifice.

The debate ranged widely over many issues, but mostly over the motives of the samurai, whether they were truly unselfish. The controversy even divided members of the same school, to say nothing of opposing schools. Of particular interest to us here is the issue of the samurai's sense of personal honor and loyalty to their lord versus the shogunate's claim to higher authority and loyalty, as if it represented public order.

In this particular case the issue arose over an alleged insult to the honor of one lord by another representing the shogunate in ritual matters. We recall the shogunate's earlier arrogation to itself of authority in matters of ritual, even in regulations for the imperial court. Implicit in this was a claim—remarkable for a shogunal regime whose *raison d'etre* was military—to civil authority through its ordering of ritual. In this respect it was performing a characteristically Confucian civil function, and one that would normally have been associated with the Imperial Court and its "civil" nobility *(kuge)*. In other words, the shogunate was using its patronage of Confucianism and appropriation of ritual functions to dignify and legitimize itself beyond its customary role of "barbarian subduing generalissimo." Understandably then, those who took the shogunate's part expressed their concern over the issue of maintaining some overall public authority, whereas those who endorsed the action of the forty-seven *rōnin* tended to uphold the earlier medieval code of personal honor, with its cult of ritual suicide as appealing to a higher ultimate value, which one might well call religious.

This view of the forty-seven *rōnin* as acting according to a distinctly Japanese tradition was noted by Dazai Shundai (1680–1747), a student of Ogyū Sorai and someone well-grounded in Chinese studies. He wrote: "For samurai of this Eastern country[9] there is an indigenous Way: if a samurai sees his lord murdered, he immediately loses all self-control and becomes crazed for revenge. Without thought about right or wrong, he immediately jumps into the fray, believing that it is only through death that he can demonstrate his righteousness."[10] While noting this as a Japanese trait, Shundai did not condone it, arguing instead that the leader of the forty-seven *rōnin* actually acted out of selfish motives, not truly honorable ones.

This issue was recognized later by the Meiji period champion of the modern "enlightenment," Fukuzawa Yukichi (1830–1901), who identified himself with the cause of establishing public authority and maintaining a civil society in Japan. He wrote:

[P]rivate vengeance is evil. . . . In no instance can even the son of the murdered parent take it upon himself to kill this criminal in place of the government. This would be to mistake his duty as a subject of the nation, and to violate his contract made with the government. If the government disposes of the case with undue favoritism to the accused, the son should complain of this injustice to the government. Whatever the reasons one may have, one is not entitled on any account to initiate the process of punishment. Even if the murderer of one's parents is lingering before one's own eyes, one has no right to retaliate privately. . . .

While they were citizens of the state, the *rōnin* chose to ignore the importance of the laws of the land. Instead they madly murdered Lord Kira. In doing so, they misunderstood their responsibilities as citizens, they violated the rights of the government, and privately tried to pass judgment on people's crimes. Fortunately the Tokugawa government sentenced these rebellious men to death, thus settling the matter. If the government had forgiven the Akō samurai, however, then the retainers of the Kira family would have taken revenge. One vendetta would have followed another until all family and friends on both sides had been annihilated. Such a process would have reduced society to a state of lawless anarchy. Such is the harm of private vigilante justice to the state. Such lack of respect must not be allowed.[11]

By the time Fukuzawa wrote, the situation in Japan had changed radically. Commodore Perry had opened Japan, the imperial restoration had taken place, and the Tokugawa shogunate was no more. Fukuzawa's reference to "the responsibilities of citizens" reflects his awareness that Western models have come to rival Chinese ones, and the concept of citizenship in a modern state has been advanced as an alternative both to the indigenous lord/vassal or the Confucian ruler/minister (ruler/subject) relationship.

A one-time supporter of the shogunate, Yokoi Shōnan (1809–1869), who had become an ardent exponent of reform along Western lines, expressed the new view in language similar to that of the Confucian classics but also reminiscent of Shōtoku's Constitution when it asserted the claims of a universal state as representing the public interest.

Yokoi despaired of the effete leadership in both Qing China and Tokugawa Japan, and deplored the scholarship of his day, which he criticized as too bookish, antiquated, and passive in responding to the challenge of the times. Instead, the more he studied the West the more he became convinced that it embodied in many ways the humane values and activism of the early sage-kings Yao, Shun, and Yu, who were directly engaged in meeting the needs of the people, rather than in lofty theorizing or in bookish scholarship. From this standpoint, Shōnan could view a general like George Washington as more closely resembling the sages in serving the common good than the decadent rulers of China and Japan, limited by a narrow vision and corrupted by a self-centered, effete complacency. Even the Confucian value of public discussion, or discourse concerning the common good *(kōgi)*, he came to believe, was better served by the political institutions of the United States and England.

This same impulse to "restore the ancient order," however had earlier inspired Song Neo-Confucian reformers to reject the anodyne and amoral influence of Buddhism in order to press for radical political change. Thus it is significant that Shōnan, at this time, was also impressed by the strong moral stance and social teachings of Christianity, which he contrasted to Buddhist emptiness and antinomianism.

The following excerpts are taken from policy recommendations he made to Matsudaira Shungaku, Lord of Echizen, in 1860. The focus of his three theses is on economic and military reform and the cultivation of the samurai as a leadership class. Although these recommendations are nominally directed to his lord and local domain, when Shōnan speaks of "Enriching the State" (his first thesis) he is addressing the needs of Japan as a whole; "state" *(koku)* here means not just feudal state, but "country," and he sees this in the context of the larger world. Hence in the Neo-Confucian paradigm of self/family/state and "all-under-Heaven," instead of starting his presentation with self-cultivation (as one would with Zhu Xi's formula of "self-cultivation for the governance of men"), Shōnan reverses the order, establishing first a larger world-context in which to define the state and self. Many of his theses are devoted to opening up this larger perspective—as the Chinese scholar Wei Yüan had sought to expand Chinese horizons in the 1840s.

On this basis Shōnan argues that the common good (the ultimate criterion of Neo-Confucian self-cultivation and governance) can only be met through a policy of "enriching the country" by opening it up to trade and economic growth for the benefit of the people as a whole, not just to serve the narrow "selfish" interests of the feudal family domain.

Having established this larger context of "all-under-Heaven," in which economics and military power now play so large a role, Shōnan then returns to the matter of the self-cultivation of the samurai. In the third of his theses, "The Way of the Samurai (shidō)," he argues that self-cultivation of the mind-and-heart, combining the feudal military virtues with Confucian civil cultivation, is the key to human governance.

In our country from the middle ages wars have followed in succession, the Imperial Court has become weak, and various lords have parceled out groups of provinces, each defending his own territory while attacking others in turn. The people were looked upon as so much waste, and the severity of forced labor and the arbitrary collection of military rations knew no bounds. Good government was swept away from the land; it was a period in which one who was skilled in warfare became a great lord and one who was clever in strategic planning became a renowned minister.

As a result, those who are known as great ministers in the shogunate and in each of the provinces have not all been able to disentangle themselves from the old ways of national seclusion. They have devoted themselves to their lords and their provinces, while their feelings of love and loyalty for the most part ignore the virtues of the good life and on the contrary invite the resentment of the people. All this leads to troubles in ruling the land. Japan has been split up thusly and lacks a unified system. . . .

Under the system of national seclusion Japan sought safety in isolation. Hence she experienced no wars or defeats. However, the world situation has undergone vast changes. Each country has broadly developed enlightened government.

In America three major policies have been set up from Washington's presidency on: First, to stop wars in accordance with divine intentions, because nothing is worse than violence and killing among nations; second, to broaden enlightened government by learning from all the countries of the world; and third, to work with complete devotion for the peace and welfare of the people by entrusting the power of the president of the whole country to the wisest person instead of transmitting it to the son of the president, and by not having ministers bound in service to the ruler, they endeavor to work together with one aim: to achieve peace and serve the common good. All methods of administrative laws and practices and all men who are known as good and wise throughout the world are put into the country's service and a very beneficial administration—one not solely in the interest of the rulers—is developed. . . .

In England the government is based entirely on the popular will, and all government actions—large and small—are always debated by the people. . . .

As can be seen in [Zhu Xi's] preface to the *Great Learn-*

ing, the main idea of schools in the three ancient dynasties of China was to teach the way of "self-discipline for the governance of men" which began with such household duties as "sprinkling and sweeping, and responding to others," all based on the individual's moral nature, with each person exerting himself to fulfill his proper function, and without any compulsion whatever being exerted on each other.[12]

By contrast, in schools today the classics and histories are memorized and discussed, and the [separate] military arts are practiced.

To pursue the underlying principles of the moral nature and correct one's conduct in accordance with the Way is the civilizing function of letters; to control the mind-and-heart and discipline one's impetuosity, and to test these in skilled practice so as to accomplish worthy deeds, is the function of the military arts. . . .

Teachings on rulership should follow the example of the three ancient dynasties of China, during which there were great sages above and many wise men under them. As a result of these teachings, the school system also aided in rulership and produced men of character and ability. Even if the ability and virtues of rulers and ministers today do not equal those of these earlier dynasties, there is no alternative to setting up the teachings of the ancients as goals. Hence rulers and ministers both must realize that they cannot depart from the unified way of civil and military arts. . . .[13]

At the time Shōnan wrote these lines, he was still hoping that the court and shogunate would work together to deal with the West, but for his model he looks to the West for an example of rule in the public interest to remedy the long process of privatization that had debilitated Japan, and to re-enliven the dominant mode of leadership.

8

Citizen and Subject in Modern Japan

With the Meiji Restoration of 1868 and the commitment to build a modern state, a new idea of citizenship took hold, and as Fukuzawa Yukichi proposed, it was to be implemented directly by and in the service of a state claiming to advance the public good, according to the standards of modern civilization and a new civility. The question then arose of how the new citizenship, as participating in the new political order, would relate to earlier concepts of leadership, possibly drawing on the feudal code of the samurai elite or the Neo-Confucian civil learning of the "noble man," or to concepts of civility as found on the local level in the popular morality propagated by Neo-Confucian teachers in the seventeenth and eighteenth century.

The term "Meiji" in the common expressions Meiji Restoration (1868) and Meiji Period (1868–1911) means "enlightened rule." Here enlightenment has some associations with the Neo-Confucian cultivation of the moral and rational nature, as in the "luminous virtue" (*meitoku*) of the *Great Learning.* Conversely, this enlightened rule has little or no connection with the alternative conception of enlightenment as found in Buddhist *satori*. More important than either of these possibilities, in a period of rapid modernization, it was with the enlightenment of the eighteenth- and nineteenth-century West that the Meiji enlightenment became strongly identified. Of this westernized view Fukuzawa Yukichi was a prime exponent in the 1870s.

In his *Outline of a Theory of Civilization* (1875) articulating a new progressive and millenarian view of world history, Fukuzawa did not picture the West as necessarily the very pinnacle of civilized development, but only as representing in the nineteenth century the most advanced stage of a broader human development that would culminate one day in a utopian fulfillment:

> When we are talking about civilization in the world today, the nations of Europe and the United States of America are the most highly civilized, while the Asian countries, such as Turkey, China, and Japan, may be called semideveloped countries, and Africa and Australia are to be counted as still primitive lands. . . .
>
> When, several thousand years hence, the levels of knowledge and virtue of the peoples of the world will have made great progress (to the point of becoming utopian), the present condition of the nations of the West will surely seem a pitifully primitive stage. Seen in this light, civilization is an open-ended process. We cannot be satisfied with the present level of attainment of the West. . . .
>
> Civilization is not a dead thing; it is something vital and moving. As such, it must pass through sequences and stages; primitive people advance to semideveloped forms, the semideveloped advance to civilization, and civilization

itself is even now in the process of advancing forward. . . . Since this is true in all countries of the world, be they primitive or semideveloped, those who are to give thought to their country's progress in civilization must necessarily make European civilizations the basis of discussion and must weigh the pros and cons of the problem in the light of it. . . .

The more social intercourse there is, the more citizens of a nation meet one another; the more human relationships broaden and their patterns evolve, so much more will human nature become civilized and human intelligence develop. Hence the term *civilization* in English.[1]

Fukuzawa did not see all wisdom as necessarily coming from the West, nor the East as lacking altogether in men of learning and virtue. Rather, the key difference between the two lay in the general level of culture among the people and how its extension enables the people as a whole to maximize the exercise of virtue in public life and minimize the effects of ignorance and incompetence.

To say that the West is civilized and Asia uncivilized means that in the West the very stupid cannot give free rein to their stupidity and that in Asia the very outstanding cannot give free rein to their knowledge and virtue. This is because civilization is not a matter of the knowledge or ignorance of individuals but of the spirit of entire nations. Thus we can judge a nation as civilized only by considering the spirit that pervades the whole land. This "spirit" is a manifestation of the knowledge and virtue of the entire population. . . . (47)

To raise the general level of knowledge and virtue so that it could exert itself on the leadership level through the mobilization of public opinion was for Fukuzawa the key to en-

gendering the new spirit of civility essential to the advance
of civilization in the East.

> Try to trace the origins of public opinion and you will find it
> an impossible task; it seems to come out of nowhere, yet it
> has the power to control the affairs of government. The rea-
> son the government cannot handle its affairs is not some
> fault of a handful of officials but this public opinion. When
> the mass of society is in error, one should not put the blame
> on the policies of officials. The ancients felt the necessity of
> first rectifying the ruler's mind, but my idea is different.
> The most urgent national task is to rectify the ills of public
> opinion. Since officials are the ones who have closest con-
> tact with national problems, they should naturally have the
> strongest concern of the country and be sufficiently worried
> about public opinion to seek ways to rectify this opinion.
> This is not what happens, however. . . . These men are in a
> position in which they are supposed to worry about the peo-
> ple under them, but instead they do things that cause peo-
> ple to worry about them. (61)

It is not difficult to see in Fukuzawa's special emphasis
on the role of "public opinion" a recognition (similar to that
of his somewhat earlier contemporary, Nakae Chōmin) that
the essential element in remedying Japan's weaknesses
versus the West lay in stimulating more active participation
of the people as a whole in public discussion focused on the
common good. A greater concern for civility as the spiritual
basis of a higher civilization, achieved through raising the
level of public opinion, became the great aim of Fukuzawa
as a citizen of the new age as he promoted those systemic
elements of a civil society identified with public discourse.
Indeed, Fukuzawa, eschewing political office, made it his

primary role to serve as an independent educator and publicist.

Another prominent thinker of somewhat contrasting ideas was Nakamura Masanao (1832–1890). An active contributor to the Enlightenment debates in the Meiji Six Journal *(Meiroku zasshi)*, Nakamura was distinctive among the promoters of the Enlightenment movement by his study of Neo-Confucianism under Satō Issai at the shogunal school, the Shōheikō. Satō reflected the late Tokugawa trend toward synthesis of Zhu Xi and Wang Yangming. The strong emphasis of this approach on the morally responsible self and dedicated activism may help to explain why Nakamura was attracted to Protestant Christianity and became a translator of Samuel Smiles' *Self-help* as well as of John Stuart Mill's *On Liberty,* both of them widely influential in promoting modern Western ideas in Meiji Japan.

No doubt still influenced by his early Neo-Confucian training, Nakamura saw many correspondences between Confucian tradition and the modern Western values he came to espouse. This contrasted with the thinking of Fukuzawa Yukichi in his early phase, whose advocacy of Western civilization, progress, and modernization implied a strong break with tradition. Thus the two were often seen as at opposite poles. Nakamura, too, was familiar with Western civilization, especially with post-Reformation and Enlightenment movements in Europe, but saw himself as basically looking for common human ground on which to reconcile Western traditions and Confucian values as a whole.

In a speech of April 1890 entitled "Past-Present, East-West: One Morality" he offered reflections on East-West values that can be taken as long-term tendencies predisposing him both to accept new ideas and to see in them confirmation of underlying human values common to China, Japan, and the West.

In discussing similarities and differences among things, each is a distinct case. In comparing them, there is the objective of acknowledging the points they have in common—for example, when one says that even though men and women are different they are alike as humans, one speaks in recognition of the similarities. When one says that even though men and women are both human, still their natures differ in regard to firmness and softness, this is to acknowledge the differences. Thus, there are times when one acknowledges similarities using generalizations and synthesis, and other times when one recognizes differences using analysis. Even though, in teaching, a thousand similarities and ten thousand differences could be cited, in order to lead all people to the good, one emphasizes the similarities and talks in generalizations. . . .

What I will discuss today is the essential unity of East and West in basic morality. It is a case of what I have called acknowledging similarities and achieving synthesis. In such a discussion, however, there are times when one must also compare and analyze, and one cannot simply generalize. But today, my aim is to set aside small differences and stress large similarities, to do away with a narrow view and approach the large view of those of consummate achievement. . . .

Moral virtue inheres in people naturally. It is a natural endowment from Heaven. From this naturally good knowledge and ability[2] in the people comes good conduct. . . . Therefore regardless of whether it is past or present, East or West, North or South, in all times, all places—this inherent moral virtue and basis of moral conduct, is common to all.

There is overall great similarity and little difference [among humankind].

Nakamura then contrasts those universal human values with the seeming amorality of a view of evolution based on the survival of the fittest, but he rejects the idea that this latter view is necessarily characteristic of the West.

In this survival of the fittest situation, force becomes inevitable. It is as if morality and humaneness are being swept away like dust from the face of the earth and rather than emphasizing morality, people think they should display military might and assert themselves by force. . . .

When generalizing about the various countries of the West today, it is a mistake to say that they are immoral. When generalizing about the various countries of the West today, it is a mistake to say they are hellish realms, full of bloodshed and fighting. Overall, it is a mistake to say that the countries of the West are ruled by force. When looking at the various countries of the West today, can we not say they are prosperous and have strong armies? And can we not say they have great power to overwhelm Asia? Is this prosperity and strength accidental? There is a cause, if we examine this closely we will surely know that [in the various Western countries] there is a base of morality, a trunk of wisdom, and a flowering of learning. Today the prosperity and strength they have harvested are the fruits of this [morality and learning]. . . .

In the West, the individual (independent self) and sociality (human relations) are the two main pillars standing together. Around these two elements one's life is built. This sociality of human relations is a characteristic unique to mankind. We associate with others, sharing joys and sorrows, sharing fortune and misfortunes. Nevertheless this is secondary. The independent self within each person is the basis of morality, that is to say, the self is to be regarded as fundamental. . . . Since the choice of accepting or disregarding the good and evil in them is up to the freedom of each individual, the words or actions of the heart and mind all belong to the individual. Because they are based on the self, the responsibility for them also unavoidably reverts to the self. Again, response to or retribution for moral goodness or sin is something that returns to each individual. This then is the way of the principle of freedom. One will surely be able to see the resultant prosperity and peace in a society or a country that gathers together the good virtues of independent individuals to create a society. . . .

As far as individual morality is concerned, regardless of past and present, East or West, in the end, the main principle is one thing called self-governance. . . .

This self-governance, is, in other words, the central concern of the above-mentioned independent self and is the source of the principle of freedom (independence). . . .

In the above discussion, there is no freedom to be found apart from the moral person, and without freedom one is unable to choose goodness. Without freedom one cannot be resolute and at ease. To enlarge upon this discussion, [I will use the ideas of a] Western scholar who states that, this thing called freedom means to be the master of oneself. This closely resembles the earlier teaching in China that one should "be discriminating, keep to unity [what is common or shared] and hold to the Mean."[3] Moreover, this corresponds to the Song Confucian understanding which emphasized the Mind of the Way as master and the mind of man which is to obey Heaven's imperative [in the mind of the Way]. . . .[4] Is it not the kind of freedom that involves choosing the good such as was said of Yan Hui: "Yan Hui [only had] a handful of rice, a gourdful of water, lived in a humble lane [and yet his joy was] unaltered."[5] If this is not the freedom to choose the common good, as in "choosing the Mean and obtaining the one good,"[6] then what is it?

To sum this up in a few words, the true meaning of the Western philosophy of freedom, in Chinese terms, is to gain freedom by making the Mind of the Way [Heaven's principles] one's master and not being a slave to the human mind [conflicted by selfish desire]. This thing, freedom, is actually the basis of self-cultivation, that is, the root of self-governance. It is precisely in this that the origin of well-being lies as well as the foundation of family and state. This is one preeminent aspect of the view that the morality of past and present, East and West is one. . . .

One's conscience and loving feeling, being rooted in human nature are the main basis of morality as understood in past and present, East and West—what we have referred to as largely one and the same, with large similarities and small differences.[7]

Here Nakamura links Yen Hui's choosing virtue over personal comfort (in *Analects* 6:9) and Zhu Xi's choosing the common or public good (keeping to unity and the Mean, in his preface to the *Mean*) to the freedom of moral choice which is the root of self-governance, East and West. Classical Confucianism and Neo-Confucianism are thus one in the exercise of moral virtue on behalf of both self-governance and the common good—a fundamental value in the West as well. On this ground he is ready to generalize about "One Morality" as the basis of the new Enlightenment.

At about this same time (1890) the Meiji government was in the process of promulgating its Imperial Rescript on Education, the language of which also drew on Confucian moral discourse but to somewhat different effect.

This Rescript was the product of a complex institutional and ideological sorting-out that followed the adoption of a Western-style school system in the 1870s. Frequently described as the outcome of a successful campaign by conservative moralists to reassert traditional values against the influences of an insurgent progressivism, it actually emerged as a consensus document from a process of consultation and contestation among Confucian advisers to the throne (principally Motoda Eifu and Nishimura Shigeki); Western-oriented educators; conservatives; progressives; cabinet members under Yamagata Aritomo; and prefectural governors concerned over the erosion of public morality on both the local and national level. The resultant mix contained a core of simple, homespun ethical precepts (which could be taken as either "Confucian" or "universal human" values, as one preferred) combined with elements of a new imperial ideology centered on the concept of "national polity (*kokutai*)."

Labeled as a "rescript," this document was not meant to function as formal law, but as instruction from on high, couched in the succinct, aphoristic style of the "classic" and the portentous language of sacred utterance. It reads:

Know ye, Our subjects:

Our Imperial Ancestors (*waga kōso kōsō*) have founded Our Empire on a basis broad and everlasting and have deeply and firmly planted virtue. Our subjects ever united in loyalty (*chū*) and filial piety (*kō*) have from generation to generation illustrated the beauty thereof. This is the glory of the fundamental character of Our Empire (*kokutai no seika*), and herein also lies the source of Our education (*kyōiku no engen*). Ye, Our subjects, be filial to your parents, affectionate to your brothers and sisters; as husbands and wives be harmonious, as friends true; bear yourselves in modesty and moderation; extend your benevolence to all; pursue learning and cultivate arts, and thereby develop intellectual faculties and perfect moral powers; furthermore advance public good and promote common interests; always respect the Constitution and observe the laws. Should emergency arise, offer yourselves courageously to the State (*giyūkō ni hōshi*); and thus guard and maintain the prosperity of Our Imperial Throne coeval with Heaven-and-earth. So shall ye not only be Our good and faithful subjects (*chūryō no shinmin*), but render illustrious the best traditions of your forefathers.

The Way here set forth is indeed the teaching bequeathed by Our Imperial Ancestors, to be observed alike by Their Descendants and the subjects, infallible for all ages and true in all places. It is Our wish to lay it to heart in all reverence, in common with you, Our subjects, that we all thus attain to the same virtue.[8]

The middle portion of the text (and its ethical core) is indeed traditional and comes originally from Zhu Xi's precepts for village instruction and community compacts, which, by a long, circuitous process, had become staples in Edo period village and family instruction. In Zhu Xi's original instructions, however, the emphasis was on filial piety, respect for elders, brotherliness, vocational commitment, and learning—virtues applicable to all members of a family or community, irrespective of class or status, to which hardly anyone would object. Significantly, there was no reference whatever in the original to ruler, state, or "loyalty" as a supposed Confucian virtue. These elements became piggy-backed onto the original precepts only later, when Zhu Xi's formulation was coopted by the founding emperor of the Ming and later amended by Qing rulers for their own imperial purposes, focused more on the state than the local community. In this late Meiji version, the original core has become encased in a new Japanese imperial ideology.

As a combination of familiar ethical platitudes and patriotic sentiments, this consensus document won acceptance from many quarters in the 1890s, as well as resistance from some independents like the Christian Uchimura Kanzō. But a strong nationalist twist was given to it by the widely disseminated commentary of Inoue Tetsujirō (1855–1944), a prominent proponent of Confucian philosophy and critic of Western liberal influences. His interpretations were cast in the standard Neo-Confucian genre of Extended Meaning *(engi),* long associated with adaptations of Zhu Xi's original Six Precepts. Inoue's Extended Meaning, a modernized and Japanized one incorporating Western concepts of the organic state and survival of the fittest, reads in part:

In the world today Europe and America are of course great powers, while the countries settled by the Europeans have all prospered as well. Now only the countries of the East are capable of competing with the progress of these nations. Yet, India, Egypt, Burma, and Annam have already lost their independence; Siam, Tibet, and Korea are extremely weak and will find it difficult to establish their autonomy. Thus in the Orient today Japan and China alone have an independence stable enough to vie for rights with the powers. But China clings to the classics and lacks the spirit of progress. Only in Japan does the idea of progress flourish, and Japan has it within its means to anticipate a glorious civilization in the future.

Japan, however, is a small country. Since there are now those that swallow countries with impunity, we must consider the whole world our enemy. Although we should always endeavor to conduct friendly relations with the powers, foreign enemies are watching for any lapse on our part, and then we can rely only upon our forty million fellow countrymen. Thus any true Japanese must have a sense of public duty, by which he values his life lightly as dust, advances spiritedly, and is ready to sacrifice himself for the sake of the nation.

But we must encourage this spirit before an emergency occurs. "Making a rope to catch a thief only after he shows up" is obviously foolish. The purpose of the Rescript is to strengthen the basis of the nation by cultivating the virtues of filiality and fraternal love, loyalty and sincerity *(kōtei chūshin)* and to prepare for any emergency by nurturing the spirit of collective patriotism *(kyōdō aikoku)*. If all Japanese establish themselves by these principles, we can be assured of uniting the hearts of the people.[9]

In the promulgation of the Imperial Rescript we witness an imperial takeover of Zhu Xi's concise ethical code, originally communitarian and remaining so in the hands of a conscientious Neo-Confucian like Muro Kyūsō, but now recast in a manner quite similar to the Imperial Confucianism of the Sacred Edict in Qing China. A further official iteration of this new pseudo-Confucian ideology, *Fundamentals of Our National Polity,* was published in the 1930s as an accompaniment to the Japanese military's expansionist moves in East Asia.[10] We conclude this discussion of the melding of modern and classic ideas by citing a work by a major figure in Japanese philosophy, Watsuji Tetsurō (1899–1960), whose "The Way of the Japanese Subject" covers much of the same ground as the *Fundamentals of our National Polity* but also gives a convenient historical résumé of many of the same developments we have been recounting here.

In the Japanese title of the work, *Nihon no shindō, shin* is the same word as the one we have seen variously rendered: in Chinese contexts most often as minister, and in Japanese as vassal, retainer, or samurai. In the late nineteenth, early twentieth-century development of a populist nationalism, the "people" are endowed with the status of samurai, converted from passive subjects to active participants in a new imperial state, expected to serve with the same self-sacrificing loyalty as the former samurai. Here "everyman" *(min)* is being mobilized as a samurai-subject into a "national people" *(kokumin)* serving the Emperor.

Watsuji claims that the absolute loyalty of this new subject is an organic and logical development from Japan's original imperial roots, reinforced later by Buddhism (especially Zen) and a Confucianism transformed by *bushidō* in the late medieval and Edo periods. Needless to say this is at a considerable remove from Mencius' earlier concept of the loyal minister who is willing to risk death in remonstrating with the ruler.

> The practice of the samurai was expressed in the moral sentiment that he "should not regret giving his life for his lord." As described repeatedly in such things as the medieval war tales, the warriors of eastern Japan truly abandoned their lives in a dauntless spirit. This was indeed a magnificent ethic that can still be appreciated. But on those occasions the "lord" referred to was the lord of one's own domain or, in the highest case, the Shogun, one of his direct retainers, or a lower shogunal official. The samurai in this way were sacrificing their lives within a system of vertical feudal relations. Consequently, even if they said they were attacking an enemy, it was in the context of the necessities of medieval civil warfare. In such a situation, if their sense of love and gratitude toward their lord was extremely

powerful, no reflection might arise as to what they were giving their lives for. If those samurai began to reflect on the significance of the death-defying duty they undertook, they would perhaps have become confused on the issue. And, in point of historical fact, this gave rise to two tendencies in the late Muromachi period. On the one hand, within the samurai class there arose a tendency referred to as "the lower overcoming the higher" (gekokujō) [upsetting the vertical hierarchical relations] and superseding one's lord. But, on the other hand, some of them sought a deeper point than the feudal vertical system of loyalties for the significance of casting away one's life. This latter tendency gave rise to the Way of Venerating the Emperor (sonnō) that was an ancient cultural legacy from the beginnings of the Japanese nation. And this latter code of honor came to blend with a deepening understanding of Buddhism or Confucianism as the samurai's code of belief. All of these motivations caused the samurai to embody a consciousness that transcends death and life. . . .

For convenience of discussion, let me first take up the connection of these ideas with Buddhism. The fundamental force that created what is known as Kamakura period Buddhism was this standpoint of the warrior who willingly sacrifices his life for his lord. Kamakura period Buddhism undoubtedly represents a Japanization of Buddhism. . . . However, the initial feudal standpoint of willingly sacrificing one's life for one's lord that accompanied this important cultural development in Kamakura Buddhism ripened, through a process of further historical mediation, into the deeper standpoint of transcending death and life. The samurai consciousness matured into an absolute consciousness incomparably greater than their sense of their own individual lives and loyalties.

It was Zen that was deeply linked to the life of the warriors at this stage, permeating every corner of it. For example, it was Zen that permeated their art of swordsmanship. Because the art of swordsmanship is a discipline of killing an enemy, a Westerner might think that it was totally unconnected with religion. But, as a matter of fact, the Japanese samurai experienced the consummation of their art of the sword precisely in the teachings of Zen. Hence the literature is replete with such phrases as "the unity of Zen and the sword." . . .

Next, I should like to consider the connection between the idea of dying and Confucianism. This was not an original strain in Chinese Confucianism. It was the Japanese samurai who gave shape to the concept from within their own experience. The connection with Confucianism came later. As mentioned above, the code of the samurai *(bushidō)* could not attain an ideal resolution in the system of vertical relationships with their feudal lords. In due course, as the samurai class acquired a more profound sense than this vertical form of loyalty to their lords, their own raw struggles for power among themselves gave rise to the sense of another way—a way that was independent of the system of feudal hierarchies. They came to respect the sheer act of courage in itself entailed in sacrificing their lives without personal regrets. . . . They would freely cast aside even their own lives in order to preserve their courage, purity of intention, and nobility of spirit. It was here that they discovered a more precious value than their own lives—the direct opposite of the attitude of preserving one's own life at all costs. In this process of historical evolution, the standpoint that transcends death and life resurfaced. The senses of dignity and of honor that emerged from this standpoint in the samurai of the late Muromachi period were then clearly linked to Confucianism as it began to gain prominence at the beginning of the Edo period. . . .

Confucianism basically expounds a morality of the Confucian gentleman motivated by benevolence or humanity (*jen*). The literal meaning of the Confucian noble man (*junzi*) concept meant one who was in the position of governing the common people. But the Japanese expounded a philosophy of the superior man's embodying the Way of Confucius, and they further equated this with the Way of the Warrior. The samurai class was taking on civil status and functions. . . . In this way, *bushidō* came to be recognized as a living embodiment of the Confucian Way—a Way that was grasped as more valuable than life itself. . . .

[This] was at first mediated as a purely formal Confucian concept; consequently, it gained currency not as the theory of Veneration of the Japanese Emperor (*sonnō*) but merely that of venerating one's lord (*son'ō*). . . .

The Way of Veneration of the Emperor had in fact been an unbroken thread of thought from the very beginning of Japanese history, taking root deeply in the lives of the Japanese people. Even in the periods in which the samurai were preoccupied with their own system of direct feudal relations, the spirit of Veneration of the Emperor existed in the depths of its heart. . . .

Insofar as this standpoint of Veneration of the Emperor embodies the absolute in the Japanese nation, it is far more concrete than the so-called world religions. But again, insofar as it does not make the absolute into a specific God, it stands on a far loftier level than the world religions. Therefore it is able to blend tolerance with any kind of religion, even while shining forth in its own brilliance and august dignity. . . .

One of the reasons the samurai class subordinated Buddhism to Confucianism three hundred years ago lies herein. However much Zen taught the samurai about an absolute state of existence, they could not allow Zen's accompanying disparagement of the moral domain. This perception was a correct one. Their entering into a state of absolute existence and their serving the Emperor had to be directly one process. . . . The true destruction of the self is certainly not realized in a standpoint wherein one thinks of the private interests of one's class, party, or group. A task ordered by the Emperor is a public task, a national task, concerning which there should be no admixture or adulteration of selfish or partisan interest. In carrying out such a public task, destruction of the egotistic self involves thoroughly realizing a condition that transcends death and life. The most important matter is that the duty of the subject is a public duty which stands above the people and governs them. This is the basic meaning of subject *(omi/shin)* as distinguished from people *(tami/min).* . . .

This, then, is the Way of the Japanese Subject, a way already grasped by our ancestors more than one thousand years ago. Thereafter, as the Way of the Warrior based in their system of vertical relationships in the separate feudal domains, it passed through various fires until it has now finally crystallized into an unparalleled beautiful jewel on the world-historical stage of today.[11]

In sum, as Watsuji presents the new "Japanese subject" as successor to "the people" *(min)*, the subject has become heir to the self-sacrificial duty of the samurai—a religious duty that transcends all notions of ordinary civility and fails to mention any of the ways in which the subject might participate as a citizen in a new political process. Thus we end here on a note far different from that of Yoshino Sakuzō, who (in 1916) had raised the question of the political morality that should inform a new parliamentary democracy .

It is evident that Watsuji's conception of the Way of the Subject *(Shindō)* follows the earlier equation of *shin* with samurai and of lord with Emperor, calling on the subject to adhere to a traditional veneration of the Emperor and a practice of *bushidō* understood as a feudal ethic strongly infused by Zen. Confucianism had little to do with it, being subsumed under the Way of the Warrior—not the Confucian Way Nakae Tōju had advocated.

In the thinking of Watsuji's contemporary, Yoshino Sakuzō, whose views on constitutionalism (cited in Chapter 1) are the touchstone in this discussion, the position of the Emperor in Japanese tradition loomed no less large than it did for Watsuji. Yoshino, however, aligned himself with the side of the Japanese tradition symbolized by Prince Shōtoku and the Meiji Emperor—that is, with the Emperor as sage ruler guided by the advice of others in the Confucian vein. Moreover, as a Japanese Christian who believed in the equality and brotherhood of mankind as children of God, he unhesitatingly accepted many of the principles underlying Western democracy and parliamentarism, without any pretense that it was somehow a home-grown product.

This is evident in his straightforward advocacy of three essential provisions of a constitutional order: (1) guarantee of civil liberties; (2) the separation of the three branches of government, and (3) a popularly elected legislature—none of them having a formal or legal basis in East Asian experience.

At the same time, Yoshino insisted on two prerequisites that did have a native ring to them: the essential leadership of an educated (not a social) elite, and the need for such leaders both to exemplify and to inculcate in the people at large the public virtues essential to the workings of any government, on any level.

Some people today might see this leadership role as a form of elitism or *noblesse oblige,* and no doubt there is a link between Yoshino's Christian sense of humanitarianism and dedication, and the samurai's sense of personal commitment along with the Confucian conviction of a high calling to public service. But Yoshino clearly saw this as a vocation to educate the people at large to an informed participation in the electoral process—not as a means to perpetuate the position or privilege of an elite. In his words,

In some countries the privileged classes survive as relics of a bygone age and still continue to exercise their influence. Where this is so, even though the pressure of world trends has forced the promulgation of a constitution, there are many who try to implement it so as to do no injury to their antiquated political ideology. These people stridently emphasize the principle that their nation's constitution has nothing in common with that of any other, but instead possesses its own peculiar coloration. We frequently see the like in our country, where there is a tendency in constitutional theory to assert as the basis for the political structure a peculiar national morality of our own, attempting in this way to avoid interpreting the Constitution in accordance with Western constitutional ideas. . . . Of course, each country's constitution is tinged with that country's peculiar coloration. It would be difficult to summarize the unique qualities of each country's constitution, but it is possible to infer from the history of modern world civilization the spiritual basis common to them all. . . . The common spiritual basis which I discover in all constitutions is democracy.[12]

For Yoshino the moral and spiritual basis for this democracy is effective service to further the public welfare; that aim may be achieved to some degree by different forms of government, but is best served by parliamentary systems. How representative such systems are depends in turn on the extent and degree of the people's informed participation, and here too Yoshino lays the main burden of responsibility on educated leadership:

> [People] are prone to say that constitutional government has failed to develop as we had hoped because the thought of the people has not developed. Yet, whether or not the people's thought develops is really determined by whether or not advanced thinkers properly guide it. When the small class of leaders holds to its narrow-minded views, it is impossible to implant in the hearts of the common people sound constitutional ideas no matter how much the necessity of spreading constitutional thought is preached. In this connection I must turn to the small enlightened intellectual class in the upper ranks of society and express the hope that they themselves achieve a true understanding of constitutional ideas and become conscious of their duty to guide the common people. (730)

Here Yoshino's concern is not with the old samurai class, who had lost their hereditary status and privileges after the Meiji Restoration, but with determining whether the surviving leadership can measure up to the challenge posed by the new plutocracy. He says:

> Though in general the privileged classes have little by little come to understand the demands of the people and thus may be considered to be aware of the way in which to meet them, there are still narrow-minded persons in these classes who value themselves highly and are condescending to the people. . . . In order that the place of these classes in a democracy may be peacefully settled and a trend to-

ward a healthy development of society thereby created, it is necessary that on the one hand we work for the development of the people's knowledge and that on the other we urge the upper classes seriously to search their hearts. (51–53)

In recent times there has been a trend in our country and others toward the appearance of certain new privileged classes in addition to the historic ones, chief among these is the plutocracy. . . . It is contrary to the objective of democracy for economically superior and inferior classes to develop and as a consequence for profits to become the monopoly of a single class. Therefore, without touching on the fundamental problem of whether or not the organization of society should be basically reconstructed, it has of late been considered necessary in government to resort temporarily to moderate measures directed against these economically privileged classes. . . . To consider now the situation in our own country, in recent times capitalists have gained strength and with their huge financial power are finally on the point of wrongfully trampling upon the public interest. . . .

This kind of privileged class will in the future come into conflict with the demands of democracy; how the two will be harmonized is a matter which engages our most anxious attention. Since the moneyed class are concerned with things from a materialistic point of view, they do not readily listen to the voice of the ordinary people. Consequently, if there come to be great difficulties in solving problems in the area of [constitutional] government, will they not in all likelihood arise from this problem of the financially privileged class? (730)

One way Yoshino would deal with the exercise of influence by the financial interests *(zaibatsu)* is to adopt strict election laws and extend universal mankind suffrage so as to expand the electorate beyond the point where it could be, in effect, bought out.

When legislators manipulate the people, invariably corruption and bad government flourish. Only when the people control their legislators does the operation of constitutional government follow the proper course. Therefore, it is especially important to impose strict penalties on the corrupt practices which may be carried on between the legislators and the people. . . . In this respect, a rather strict election law has been adopted in Japan; the only thing to be regretted is that it has not been rigorously enough enforced, and that the government tends to be lax in dealing with the activities of its own party. (91–92)

If the suffrage is limited, corrupt practices are carried on unreservedly. When the suffrage is extended to the limit, there can be absolutely no distribution of bribes and the like. Moreover, only when it has become absolutely impossible for candidates to fight one another with money and things of value will they compete by sincerely and frankly presenting their views and personal qualifications to the people. Consequently, the people will gain an opportunity to receive a political education through this means. . . .

Thus, the extension of the suffrage and the strict enforcement of electoral laws are the most pressing matters facing Japan. The history of other countries shows that these two actions have often effected a clean-up in political life. If they are neglected, the ideal of constitutional government cannot be realized no matter how much one preaches about election ethics and prods the conscience of the people. (741)

As a matter of practical politics, Yoshino advocated a parliamentary system culminating in cabinets representative of the majority party, and he opposed so-called national coalitions that were supposedly above party in their dedication to the higher national interest:

> In contrast to the responsible cabinet system there is also the principle of the nonparty cabinet. According to this idea, the cabinet should rise above the wishes of parliament and occupy a position of absolute independence. Under this system, no matter how much the government is opposed by parliament, no matter even if on occasion there are votes of non-confidence [in parliament], the government unconcernedly continues in office. To put the theory in its worst light, it is a pretext which enables the government freely to perpetrate any kind of arbitrary misrule. Thus it is inconsistent with the principle that final decisions on policy should depend upon the views of the people generally. (743)

For Yoshino responsible government could best be achieved by the parliamentary cabinet system:

> In most countries it has recently become the practice for the government to be formed by the leader of the political party that has a majority in parliament. In this sense most governments are today party cabinets. . . . In countries where there are just two major parties, this system works well, but in those with many small parties, it does not. . . . In order that the wisdom of the party cabinet system may be demonstrated, it is absolutely necessary to encourage the establishment of two major parties. However, the coming into being of two major parties is a matter which is determined by the course of events, and cannot very well be controlled by a constitution's theory. As a result, the workability of the party cabinet system always varies from one country to another. Hence the problem arises as to whether party government can really work smoothly in Japan. (243)

Yoshino's analysis of the final "problem" here was both acute and prophetic. Although some of his main goals were achieved in the 1920s, a period which is usually identified with party politics, democratic movements (most specifically the achievement of universal manhood suffrage), and international foreign policy, it proved difficult to sustain a parliamentary system such as Yoshino's, based on two main political parties with stable allegiances. Coalitions negotiated among factions proved to be the rule, and while these operated on the basis of traditional consensus-building mechanisms, with their own implicit understandings and "feel" for consensus, they were also subject to pressures of the moment and changes of popular mood—not the principled basis for party platforms and policies Yoshino had hoped for.

This then left Japanese party politics susceptible to charges of corruption of all kind, but especially factional dealing, election buying, and serving the moneyed interests. Whether such corruption was more prevalent in Japan than in other democracies is arguable; it may simply have been better publicized than in more tightly controlled regimes. But it became a feature of strident protests from the extreme right, who combined Nazi-type "national socialist" attacks on capitalism and party politics with the profession of utter loyalty to the Emperor. As one striking example of this right-wing ideology we may cite the so-called Righteousness Corps of the Divine Land, a movement led by Asahi Heigo, who assassinated the *zaibatsu* leader, Yasuda Zenjirō, in 1921, and then committed suicide. To his followers he left a manifesto calling for the abolition of capitalism, crushing of the political parties, punishing of high officials (including moderate military leaders), and abolishing all provisions for the inheritance

of rank and wealth, among other radical or populist measures. Asahi concluded his manifesto:

> These are initial steps. But the punishment of the traitor-
> ous millionaires is the most urgent of all these, and there is
> no way of doing this except to assassinate them resolutely.
>   Finally, I want to say a word to my colleagues. I hope that
> you will live up to my principles. Do not speak, do not get
> excited, and do not be conspicuous. You must be quiet and
> simply stab, stick, cut, and shoot. There is no need to meet
> or to organize. Just sacrifice your life. And work out your
> own way of doing this. In this way you will prepare the way
> for the revolution. The flames will start here and there, and
> our fellow idealists will band together instantly. So forget
> about self-interest, and do not think about your own name
> or fame. Just die, just sleep. Never seek wisdom, but take
> the road of ignorance and come to know the height of great
> folly. (768–769)

The anarchist elements here ("no need to meet and organize") are of a piece with other messianic revolutionary
ideologies, as, for instance, the anarchist assumptions of
the early communist movement in China at about this time
(see the views of Li Dazhao, a founder of the Chinese Communist Party, in SCT II, 406), but the mystique of revolutionary violence, exemplified by individual acts of spectacular self-sacrifice on the part of martyrs who renounce all
reason and wisdom, has its roots in the earlier samurai tradition and cult of the warrior, as enunciated in *Hagakure*
(In the Shadow of Leaves), wherein the Zen master Yamamoto Tsunetomo said:

> It is awful if a samurai's mind gets stuck on judgments
> of right and wrong, whether something is loyal or disloyal,
> righteous or unrighteous, proper or improper, and so on. If

one just devotes oneself totally and single-mindedly to the service of one's lord, forgetting all other considerations, and cherishes one's lord without second or third thoughts, that is enough. . . .

In a normal state of mind, you cannot accomplish a great task. You must become like a person crazed. . . . As soon as discriminating thoughts arise, you will already have fallen behind.[13]

Such spectacular acts as Asahi Heigo's, followed later by the attempted coup d'états of other ultra-nationalist extremists in 1931 and 1936, succeeded in bringing an end to the party governments of the 1920s, and eventually led to Japan's engagement in the disastrous wars of the 1930s and early 1940s, which led to total defeat in 1945. War's end however, brought the enactment of a new constitution in 1946–47 which, though often spoken of as an American or MacArthur-imposed system, in fact fulfilled in most respects the aims put forth by Yoshino Sakuzō and his fellow liberals of prewar Japan.

That this constitution has survived unamended for over half a century, during which time the Japanese government has functioned well enough to sustain substantial progress in most areas of life, is attributable to more than just its own intrinsic merits; it speaks well for the adaptability of the Japanese people, also and especially for the long-standing processes of social and political consultation by which they have repeatedly coped with new crises and challenges— processes that have survived major historic changes and operated through quite diverse political systems. Liberal constitutionalists in the early twentieth century, like Minobe and Yoshino, invoked the tradition of consultation on behalf of parliamentary government, and in the postwar era the prominent historian and political thinker, Maruyama Masao, saw it as functioning even in authoritarian regimes of the late 1930s and early 1940s—indeed, as still persisting in the party politics of the 1960s. In complaining about the Kishi government's handling of protests against the U.S.–Japan Security Treaty in 1960, Maruyama said: "Democracy has been replaced by 'consultation,' the peace and harmony myth of the village community. Under Japan's wartime system this consultationism was practiced in countless consultative bodies. This was, so to speak, a totalitarianism built on consultation, so that definite responsibility for decisions vanished like the morning mist."[14]

Maruyama's characterization of a "totalitarianism built on consultation" points to an inherent ambiguity in traditional consultation and consensus-formation when considered as a form or mode of civility—a process avoiding the use of force as a means of settling human affairs. On the one hand, this process has been susceptible of cooptation by those in power, as Maruyama says. In his terms it is not so much a question of what Japanese parliamentarianism (*gikai shugi*) owes to the long-standing tradition of consultation (*giron shugi*), as the advocates of constitutionalism were wont to claim. Maruyama sees this as an unstable combination, with an amorphous, subtle, even slippery consultationism often getting the better of a more formally defined parliamentarianism or constitutionalism. In such a vague process of consultation, wherein everyone seems to share in decision-making, no one clearly decides, not even the Emperor. As Maruyama says: "Definite responsibility for decisions vanished like the morning mist."

On the other hand, consultation has smoothed the political process; it has avoided all-out confrontation and obviated the kind of violence and terror that many totalitarian regimes unleashed against the opposition. The postwar constitution of 1947 could not itself have survived had it not been for the survival into the postwar years of liberal leaders like Shidehara Kijūrō and Yoshida Shigeru, who were still on hand at a critical moment to implement it politically.

The obverse of this tendency to compromise is shown in the uncompromising stance sometimes taken by individuals who reject all concession and consultation in favor of decisive personal actions—in the 1920s and 1930s those who defied party politics and chose instead spectacular acts of heroic sacrifice and self-dramatization to accomplish their political ends. Such were the perpetrators of "government by assassination" like the aforementioned Asahi Heigo.

In the postwar period this trend was represented in a more sophisticated form by Mishima Yukio (1925–1970). A brilliant novelist and dramatist whose works won international acclaim in the 1950s and 1960s, Mishima thought of himself as an example of a Japanese tradition that combined a refined aesthetic hedonism (in contrast to what he saw as the puritanism of the West) and a mystical concept of the Imperial institution as the unifying agency of a political/cultural holism. "This culture," he said,

includes not only what may be termed works of art but also modes of action. Culture includes not only the prescribed movements of the Nō play but also the actions of the naval officer who was killed after he jumped from a human torpedo as it surfaced in the moonlit sea off New Guinea and brandished his Japanese sword over his head, as it includes all of the many last letters written by members of the Special Attack Force. Everything points to the form through which the Japaneseness of things can be glimpsed in the two aspects of the "Chrysanthemum and the Sword," from *The Tale of Genji* to the modern novel, from the *Manyōshū* to avant-garde poetry, from the Buddhist statues in the Chūsonji to contemporary culture, from the flower arrangement and tea ceremony to *kendō* and *jūdō,* and even from *kabuki* to gangster movies or from Zen to military etiquette.[15]

It is not adequate to extract from Japanese culture only its static side and to ignore its dynamic side. Japanese culture has a special tradition of transforming modes of action themselves into works of art. It is a feature of Japan that the martial arts belong to the same genre of artistic form as the tea ceremony and flower arrangement; all come into being, are continued and disappear within a short space of time. *Bushidō* is a system of making ethics beautiful or perhaps of giving ethical content to beauty; it is a union between life and art. . . .

The special features of this cultural concept correspond to the special features of the emperor system in that each successive emperor is indisputably the emperor and the relationship between him and Tenshō daijin (Amaterasu, the "Sun Goddess") is not one of original and copy. (229)

The imperial institution, as a cultural concept of this nature, satisfies the two requisites of cultural totality; temporal continuity has been preserved by religious rites, but at the same time spatial continuity at times has gone so far as to tolerate even political disorder. It is as if the most profound eroticism corresponds on the one hand to ancient theocracy while being bonded with anarchism.

"*Miyabi*" (elegance) was at once the fine flower of the

court culture and the yearning it inspired, but in times of emergency, *miyabi* might even take the form of terrorism. That is to say, the emperor, being a cultural concept, was not always on the side of state authority and order; he sometimes held out his hand to disorder . . .

The patriots who, in response to the wishes of the Emperor Kōmei carried out the incident of the Sakurada Gate (the assassination of the chief shogunal minister in 1860), were putting into practice "single-hearted miyabi," an uprising for the sake of the emperor . . . but later the [postwar] emperor system under Shōwa, adhering to the European system of constitutional monarchy, had lost the ability to understand the *miyabi* [elegance] of the February 26 (1936) incident. (244–245)

In the essay excerpted here, Mishima traces in broad strokes a clear continuity from the aesthetic culture of the Heian Court to its reenactment in the Muromachi culture—claiming for it all of the classic cachet of "flower" *(hana),* simple beauty *(waka),* and faded beauty *(sabi)*— and on to the spectacular acts of heroic bravery by individuals at the time of the Restoration, to antigovernment protests ("government by assassination") in the 1920s and 1930s, and to suicide missions in the Pacific War.

The keynote of this tradition is "elegant beauty" *(miyabi),* combining the courtly elegance of Prince Genji, represented by the chrysanthemum as the flower of this aesthetic cult, with the sword that arose from the coalescence of the refined aesthetics of the Zen arts and the growing cult of the feudal Way of the Warrior.

As Mishima not only allows but boasts, this process legitimized the use of terror in the name of the Emperor and dignified even anarchism. Such, in the longer perspective of history, was the result of the conversion of the court from a center of public authority, as Prince Shōtoku had envisaged it, through the privatization of the Heian Court nobility into a genteel cultural aristocracy and the loss of any state able to represent or advance the public good. The interests of the family at court or in the feudal domains and the personal honor of the samurai were all that mattered socially.

Parallel to this in the religious domain was an emphasis on personal faith and direct intuition at the expense of explicit doctrine, while esoteric mysteries and rituals served as instruments of legitimization in the absence of any public criteria. As shared "public" standards, then, this approach left only an indefinable good taste and aesthetic finesse—themselves strongly colored by class privilege—to command respect.

With the unity of culture and politics so understood, Mishima can proceed to speak of an elevated, mysticized Emperor as a "theocrat" exercising his right even to create anarchy, "holding out his hand to disorder." On such grounds he can acclaim the individual's challenge, in the name of an Emperor so exalted, to all public or state authority, without the need for any stated rationale, without invoking any public authority apart from the mystique and ritual of a divine imperial institution.

Finally, in 1970, Mishima acted out his idea by invading a headquarters of the Self-Defense Forces (the name of the postwar military), reading an indictment of the United States-sponsored constitution of 1947, its antiwar provisions, and its degradation of the Imperial institution, after which he committed ritual suicide.

Whatever his expectations were, Mishima, performing a

grand spectacle for the news media and thereby drawing world attention to it, did not succeed in inciting the Self-Defense Forces to any coup d'état, and so his self-sacrifice accomplished nothing either politically or culturally. In the 1920s and 1930s such dramatic challenges by rightists to the established governments did have some real effect—much for the worse—on the course of domestic and foreign policy, but they never really amounted to "government by assassination," since they fell far short of gaining control of the government. Instead, "national coalition" governments, meaning "government by consensus," came in to get the situation under some control, and continued to conduct a messy war down to its bitter end.

As regards Mishima, if one were truly looking for a "Last Samurai," it would be he. The effect of his samurai-style grandstanding has been virtually nil. Consensus politics has continued to prevail. Even the 1947 constitution, widely viewed as "U.S.-imposed" and excoriated by Mishima though it was, has continued in effect without significant amendment even in respect to its bizarre renunciation of war. The Japanese quickly learned to live with it, according to their own mode and taste for consensus politics, more for good than for ill.

Thus the other side of Japanese tradition—the more prosaic, hum-drum side of consultation and consensus formation on Shōtoku's model—has endured. True, it has had to endure also many of the same criticisms Yoshino made of it in the early days of Japanese liberal politics—its inability to sustain a reasonably coherent and consistent two-party system, its susceptibility to factionalism, patronage, collusion with the bureaucracy, and financial corruption (perhaps not much greater than in other regimes, but better publicized, more in the open, than in tightly controlled, closed societies). But Japanese governments, operating by often ineluctable processes of consultation, back-room negotiation, and consensus—not dominated by strong, charismatic leaders but depending on teamwork rather than individual stars—have managed the country well enough to achieve and sustain an impressive standard of economic wellbeing and to avoid both the violence of the prewar years and the repression of civil and human rights that has characterized strong governments elsewhere. While this success has been most notable in the economic sphere, it has hardly been less so on the cultural scene, where Japanese arts and literature have quietly asserted themselves in a manner that contrasts with the rather nondescript, lackluster style of Japanese politics.

Yet Japan has not played as prominent a role in international affairs as its economic power and cultural prestige would have seemed to warrant. There, despite brilliant individual performances in the U.N. and peacekeeping missions, like that of Ogata Sadako, the Japanese low-key teamwork in international bodies has not won the attention that the Japanese economy and arts do. This may well reflect, however, a natural limitation of the nation's particular talent for consensus building and civility on the personal level—a talent that works better in more intimate domestic settings, where common cultural and social sensibilities operate to better effect than in multicultural ones. On the world scene well-articulated public policies must take the place of implicit understandings, but Japanese foreign policy has appeared as low-key and unobtrusive as its domestic policy.

In short, the "nobility" of Prince Shōtoku's leadership

and approach to harmony—through the civility of consultation and consensus-formation—has shown itself as an enduring feature of Japanese life. Susceptible sometimes to spectacular, often dangerous, and occasionally disastrous outbursts of passionate emotion or daring individual exploits, in the end that path has prevailed over the grandiose ambition of megalomaniacs like Toyotomi Hideyoshi and the wild imaginings and posturing of imperial flower-children like Mishima Yukio.

9

"The People Renewed" in Twentieth-Century China

A representative figure in early twentieth-century China who dealt with the question of Confucian values as related to citizenship in a modern nation was Liang Qichao (1873–1929), a leading scholar, publicist, and activist on behalf of constitutional government (a role parallel to that of his contemporary in Japan, Yoshino Sakuzō). Liang, however, though a progressive thinker generally identified with reformism of a Westernizing kind, was steeped in Chinese tradition, especially Confucianism. His moral and political frame of reference, like that of his Japanese counterparts, was primarily the one drawn up in Zhu Xi's version of the Four Books, and especially *The Great Learning*. But in contrast to other East Asians (Yokoi Shōnan, for example), whose political thinking was strongly conditioned by Zhu Xi's formula of "self-discipline for the governance of men," Liang was also conscious of the necessary corrective and balance to this idea (so dependent on the heroics of individuals) in the form of institutions. This he found in the writings of Huang Zongxi and other Qing dynasty thinkers who stressed the need for institutional or systemic reform if the individual's efforts were ever to be effective.[1] But statecraft tradition was much less a part of the educated intelligence in late Qing China than the *Great Learning,* and Liang took as his point of departure the second of Zhu Xi's guidelines—"renewing the people"—and attempted to see how this could be bent to the creation of a new citizenry, educated to become active agents in a new nation.

Here "nation" itself was an important new ingredient in the thinking of Chinese intellectuals, who had tended to think of the people as subjects of an emperor and dynasty—at best, the beneficiaries of benevolent rule—but not as participating citizens of a nation. Liang therefore used the metaphor of the organic nature of the nation as the basis for a more dynamic involvement of the people in public affairs. He wrote:

A state is formed by the assembling of people. The relationship of a nation to its people resembles that of the body to its four limbs, five viscera, muscles, veins and corpuscles. It has never happened that the four limbs could be cut off, the five viscera wasted away, the muscles and veins injured, the corpuscles dried up and yet the body still live. Similarly, it has never happened that a people could be foolish, timid, disorganized and confused and yet the nation still stand. Therefore, if we wish the body to live for a long time, we must understand the methods of hygiene. If we wish the nation to be secure, rich and honored, we must discuss the way for "renewing the people." . . .

Is it enough merely to develop what we already have? No, it is not. The world of today is not the world of yesterday. In ancient times, we Chinese were people of villages instead of citizens. This is not because we were unable to form a citizenry but due to circumstances. Since China majestically used to be the predominant power in the East, surrounded as we were by small barbarian groups and lacking any contact with other large states, we Chinese generally considered our state to encompass the whole world. All the messages we received, all that influenced our minds, all the instructions of our sages, and all that our ancestors passed down—qualified us to be individuals on our own, family members, members of localities and clans, and members of the world. But they did not qualify us to be citizens of a state. . . .

The main deficiency in our citizens is their lack of public morality. . . .

Among our people there is not one who looks on national affairs as if these were ones own affairs. The significance of public morality has not dawned on us. Examining into it, however, we realize that the original basis for morality lies in its serving the interests of the group. As groups differ in their degree of barbarism or civilization, so do their appropriate morals vary. All of them, however, aim at consolidating, improving and developing the group. . . .

As to the external features of morality, they vary according to the degree of progress in each group. As groups differ in barbarism or civilization, so do their public interests and their morals. Morality cannot remain absolutely unchanged. It is not something that could be put into a fixed formula by the ancients several thousand years ago, to be followed by all generations to come. Hence, we who live in the present group should observe the main trends of the world, study what will suit our nation, and create a new morality in order to solidify, benefit and develop our group.[2]

Liang believed strongly in the need for new institutions to advance the "renewal of the people" through the dissemination of information through public media—newspapers, journals, books—and through universal schooling of the kind that Neo-Confucians had advocated but never achieved. He was also committed to constitutional government that would provide the organs through which a renewed and reeducated citizenry could express itself.

To this extent then we can say that Liang advocated many of the elements of a civil society. But in his zeal to create a new nation and a new citizenry he was apt to be somewhat dismissive of the traditional civility associated with family and the village. "In former times we were people of villages, not citizens." Sun Yat-sen, at about the same time, described the Chinese people as a "sheet of loose sand" because of their primary loyalty to clan and family and lack of national loyalty—a defect in the people which caused him to call for "the freedom of the nation" rather than "freedom for the people." Likewise Mao Zedong later saw clan and family loyalties as an obstacle to national unity and the achievement of revolutionary goals, and conducted repeated campaigns against the family system.

Reflecting on the question of civility as Zhu Xi had tried to deal with it, we recall that while some elements in his community compact were what might be called "family values," namely love for parents and siblings, the majority of the provisions went beyond family to deal with community relations, and the community compact meetings were themselves celebrations of communitarian values and local autonomy (self-sufficiency) through mutual assistance.

Another twentieth-century Chinese thinker who believed that Zhu Xi's community compact still had something to offer was Liang Shuming (1893–1988), who wrote about "Reconstructing the Community." In one sense,

Liang acknowledged, the problem in his time was construction, not re-construction, because the community compact he had in mind, following Zhu Xi's model, had always been overshadowed by the state and offered no real precedent to be reactivated. Thus he wrote:

Westerners have always had everywhere group life, beginning from religion on to economics and government, whereas the Chinese have always lacked group life; everywhere it seems the whole is broken into parts. . . .

What is meant by construction is nothing but the construction of a new structure of social organization; that is, to construct new customs. Why? Because in the past our structure of social organization was shaped out of social customs; it was not shaped out of national laws. . . .

This is a time of great distress for the Chinese, a time caught in contradiction on either side, coming and going. That is to say, on the one hand the Chinese lack group organization, and at the same time they lack the establishment of individual liberty and equality; the two [deficiencies] both urgently await being made up. But if we emphasize the aspect of liberty and equality . . . then it will be very difficult for us to attend to the aspect of combining into groups and will cause the Chinese to be even more dispersed. . . . Relational ethics should allow both aspects to be established. As a result of giving play to ethical relations, the individual will necessarily respect the group, fulfilling the requisite obligation; the group will necessarily respect the individual, according it due liberty and equality. . . .

The principle of this organization is based in China's idea of ethics. It is as if, to the five relationships of parent-child, ruler-minister, husband-wife, elder brother-younger brother, friends-and-friends, there were added a relationship of group toward member, member toward group. . . .[3]

This new organization is just the supplementation and transformation of what earlier Chinese called, "the community compact" (*xiangyue*). . . . But the community compact referred to here is not the community compact promoted in the Ming and Qing dynasties by the government using political force, rather it refers to the community compact launched in the beginning by villagers themselves at the outset in the Song dynasty. . . .

In the practice of the community compact, relying on political power will not work, promotion by private individuals also will not work, hence although in history many times there has been the intention to initiate it, in reality none of these can be considered successful. I am afraid success could only be hoped for today. We understand that to rely on political power to do things—to use the power of command and coercion, if this kind of power is used, in each step it all is mechanical. . . . Each time it goes down a level, the further by a step it is from the place where it was initiated, the more it is passive, the more it becomes mechanical, the more it lacks vitality, the more it lacks energy, the more it is unable to fit the problems. . . . The more it is unable to fit problems, the more it loses its meaning, the more it becomes useless. . . .

Our village construction [rural reconstruction] is the construction of social organization, and we often like to say that this social organization is something which grows, something which gradually unfolds, that grows from sprouts, that unfolds from hints. Its sprouts and hints are in the village and from the village will slowly unfurl to form a whole society.[4]

Needless to say neither Zhu Xi's nor Liang Shuming's Community Compacts became the model for Mao Zedong's communes, which subsequently demonstrated precisely the weaknesses Liang pointed out above—the passivity that inevitably results from "the power of command and coercion."

Coercion was not, however, a problem for Mao in his early days as a revolutionary or for other early leaders of the Chinese communist movement, who were often carried away by the romantic idealism of a world proletarian revolutionary upheaval to be accomplished with little organization. Such was the case with Li Dazhao, one of the founders of the Chinese Communist Party. He characterized the inevitable triumph of the workers' soviets in terms that resemble Asahi Heigo's euphoric call to spontaneous action, on behalf of a new imperial restoration in Japan. Li says of the revolution in the West:

All those who work should join a union and there should be a central administrative soviet in each union. Such soviets then should organize all the governments of the world. There will be no congress, no parliament, no president, no prime minister, no cabinet, no legislature, and no rule. There will be only the joint soviets of labor, which will decide all matters. All enterprises will be allowed. They will unite the proletariat of the world, and create global freedom with their greatest, strongest power of the world, and create global freedom with their greatest, strongest power of resistance: First they will create a federation of European democracies, to serve as the foundation of a world federation. This is the ideology of the Bolsheviki. This is the new doctrine of the twentieth-century revolution. . . .

    In the course of such a world mass movement, all those dregs of history that can impede the progress of the new movement—such as emperors, nobles, warlords, bureaucrats, militarism, capitalism—will certainly be destroyed as

though struck by a thunderbolt. Encountering this irresist-
ible tide, these things will be swept away one by one. . . .
Henceforth, all that one sees around him will be the trium-
phant banner of Bolshevism, and all that one hears around
him will be Bolshevism's song of victory. The bell is rung for
humanitarianism! The dawn of freedom has arrived! See
the world of tomorrow; it assuredly will belong to the red
flag! The revolution in Russia is but the first fallen leaf
warning the world of the approach of autumn. Although the
word *Bolshevism* was created by the Russians, the spirit it
embodies can be regarded as that of a common awakening
in the heart of each individual among mankind of the twentieth century. (406)

Here Li Dazhao's millenarian expectations are obviously
aroused by the Bolsheviks' success in promoting revolution
in the name of an urban proletariat. Mao Zedong, for his
part, saw a greater potential in the Chinese peasantry, as he
wrote in his famous Hunan report, expecting a revolutionary tornado to sweep all before it:

The rise of the present peasant movement is a colossal
event. In a very short time, in China's central, southern
and northern provinces, several hundred million peasants
will rise like a tornado or tempest, a force so extraordinarily
swift and violent that no power, however great, will be able
to suppress it. They will break all trammels that now bind
them and rush forward along the road to liberation. They
will send all imperialists, warlords, corrupt officials, local
bullies, and bad gentry to their graves. All revolutionary parties and all revolutionary comrades will stand before them
to be tested and to be accepted or rejected as they decide.
    To march at their head and lead them? Or to follow at
their rear, gesticulating at them and criticizing them? Or to
face them as opponents?

Every Chinese is free to choose among the three alternatives, but circumstances demand that a quick choice be made.

The main force in the countryside that has always put up the bitterest fight is the poor peasants. Throughout both the period of underground organization and that of open organization, the poor peasants have fought militantly all along. They accept most willingly the leadership of the Communist Party. (406–409)

Note here that for all the euphoria about the inevitability of the revolutionary tide sweeping the world, Mao is concerned about the matter of organization and leadership. He is not rallying samurai with sword in hand, but mobilizing peasants who need leaders, and he calls on members of the educated elite to provide that leadership, not just to practice the gentlemanly arts of the Confucian scholar. This is class struggle, in which Confucian gentility and civility have no place.

A revolution is not the same as inviting people to dinner, or writing an essay, or painting a picture, or doing fancy needlework; it cannot be anything so restrained, so calm and gentle, or so mild, kind, courteous, restrained, and magnanimous.[5] A revolution is an uprising, an act of violence whereby one class overthrows another. A rural revolution is a revolution by which the peasantry overthrows the authority of the feudal landlord class. (409)

Notwithstanding Mao's contempt for Confucian civility and moderation, and the prominence given to his anti-Confucian sentiments in the Great Proletarian Cultural Revolution of the late 1960s and early 1970s, the possibility that Maoism could have drawn subconsciously from Confucian tradition in some ways cannot be discounted. Recently the Chinese scholar Li Zehou reassessed the continuing influence of Confucian tradition and the specific Neo-Confucian influences on Mao's early education, especially the influence of the Wang Yangming school. What Li has to say about this reveals a striking similarity to the case of Mishima Yukio, who was similarly attracted to Wang Yangming, his doctrine of the unity of knowledge and action, and the heroic idealism Wang both embodied and engendered. As Li Zehou put it:

Characteristic of the school of Wang Yangming is the great stress on the dynamic nature of subjective practice (moral behavior), i.e. the unity of knowledge and action. "Knowledge that is true and genuine is action, action that is conscious and discriminating is knowledge." This means that ethics is entirely reduced to the self-conscious action of the individual. "Knowledge is necessarily action"; "innate knowledge" automatically becomes action, and conscious action is identical to knowledge. That is to say, man's true existence lies in the "innate knowledge" [expressed in] activity and only in this activity can man achieve his noumenal existence. . . .

In Wang Yangming's doctrine of the unity of knowledge and action, there is not much place left for epistemology; in a certain sense, it can even be said that epistemological questions have been eliminated. The so-called extension of knowledge is not about knowledge at all but is about moral feeling.

From the beginning, starting with Lu Xiangshan, there had been a strong emphasis on "being one's own master," "self-reliance and self-respect," the doubting of canonical authority and the opposition to blind obedience . . . and this characteristic became even more important and significant with Wang Yangming and his followers.

[This] emphasis on subjectivity and willpower influenced, to a greater or lesser extent, many men of strong purpose and lofty ideals in later generations, such as Kang Youwei, Tan Sitong, the young Mao Zedong, and Guo Moruo, who used it as a spiritual weapon or support in their battle against the old society, the old order, and the old customs. The . . . aspect of individual moral cultivation, the steeling of the will, and the spirit of militancy . . . became a factor of real significance.

Although Liu Shaoqi's *How to Be a Good Communist* [see below] and Neo-Confucianism are diametrically opposed to each other, are they really dissimilar in the way in which they establish the subjective will and a sense of moral responsibility? . . . Is there really no continuity here in regard to national tradition? . . . Is it unrelated to the Chinese nation's establishment of a subjective volitional structure in terms of high regard for moral courage and character, the desire to control the feelings by means of principle, self-restraint, and firm determination? . . . In his youth, Mao Zedong earnestly studied Neo-Confucianism with his teacher Yang Changji and even spoke approvingly of Zeng Guofan . . . He paid attention to self-improvement, the steeling of the will, and attached great importance to ideals, spiritual values, and moral achievements. Could all this have had no influence upon his later activities and ideology? (579–581)

What Li says here has primary relevance to Mao's conception of heroic revolutionary leadership and his own "cult of personality." But that such Confucian influences continued to exert themselves more broadly on what might be called "post-Confucian" Chinese Communists is suggested in the famous early tract Li refers to above, *How to Be a Good Communist,* by one of Mao's principal lieutenants in his rise to power. Liu Shaoqi (1900–1969), its author, was willing to reach back to the prime Neo-Confucian text, the *Great Learning,* as a possible model for self-cultivation and self-discipline in stimulating party activism:

> Comrades! In order to become the most faithful and best pupils of Marx, Engels, Lenin, and Stalin, we need to carry on cultivation in all aspects in the course of the long and great revolutionary struggle of the proletariat and the masses of the people. . . . We are all Communist Party members and so we have a general cultivation in common. But there exists a wide discrepancy today among our Party members. . . . Therefore, in addition to cultivation in general we also need special cultivation for different groups and for individual comrades.
>
> Accordingly, there should be different kinds of methods and forms of cultivation. For example, many of our comrades keep a diary in order to have a daily check on their work and thoughts or they write down on small posters their personal defects and what they hope to achieve and put them up where they work or live, together with the photographs of persons they look up to, and ask comrades for criticism and supervision. In ancient China, there were many methods of cultivation. There was Zengzi[6] who said: "I reflect on myself three times a day." The *Classic of Odes* has it that one should cultivate oneself "as a lapidary cuts and files, carves and polishes." Another method was "to examine oneself by self-reflection" and to "write down some mottoes on the right hand side of one's desk" or "on one's girdle" as daily reminders of rules of personal conduct. The Chinese scholars of the Confucian school had a number of methods for the rectification of the mind-and-heart, the cultivation of their body and mind. Every religion has various methods and forms of cultivation of its own. The "investigation of things, the extension of knowledge, sincerity

of thought, the rectification of the heart, the cultivation of the person, the regulation of the family, the ordering well of the state, and bringing peace for the whole world," as set forth in *The Great Learning*,[7] also means the same. All this shows that in achieving one's progress one must make serious and energetic efforts to carry on self-cultivation and study. However, many of these methods and forms cannot be adopted by us because most of them are idealistic, formalistic, abstract, and divorced from social practice. These scholars and religious believers exaggerate the function of subjective initiative, thinking that so long as they keep their general "good intentions" and are devoted to silent prayer they will be able to change the existing state of affairs, change society, and change themselves under conditions separated from social and revolutionary practice. This is, of course, absurd. We cannot cultivate ourselves in this way. We are materialists and our cultivation cannot be separated from practice.

What is important to us is that we must not under any circumstances isolate ourselves from the revolutionary struggles of different kinds of people and in different forms at a given moment and that we must, moreover, sum up historical revolutionary experience and learn humbly from this and put it into practice. . . . Our self-cultivation and steeling are for no other purpose than that of revolutionary practice.

At all times and on all questions, a Communist Party member should take into account the interests of the Party as a whole, and place the Party's interests above his personal problems and interests. It is the highest principle of our Party members that the Party's interests are supreme. (427–430)

Here Liu tries to engage the Neo-Confucian's sense of individual responsibility for the public welfare on behalf of the communist cause, but he is careful to hitch it to the party wagon instead of allowing much scope to the autonomous individual and the free exercise of his own conscience.

Nevertheless, despite Liu's clear admonition that self-cultivation was not to be directed toward the cultivation of an autonomous individual or person, and despite his caution against any individual subjectivism or idealism in order to assure that these initiatives would be directed toward service of the party, these reservations were not enough to save him later; during the Cultural Revolution Mao turned on Liu and condemned him as a capitalist-roader. Whatever the personal or political reasons for this, in Mao's mind (as in the Cultural Revolution itself) capitalist individualism, liberalism, and Confucianism were classed together as ideological bedfellows. When Mao wrote his essay "Combat Liberalism," his description of liberalism sounded much like a characterization of a moderate Confucianism:

> We advocate an active ideological struggle, because it is the weapon for achieving solidarity within the Party and the revolutionary organizations and making them fit to fight. Every Communist and revolutionary should take up this weapon.
>
> But liberalism negates ideological struggle and advocates unprincipled peace, with the result that a decadent, philistine style in work has appeared and certain units and individuals in the Party and the revolutionary organizations have begun to degenerate politically.
>
> Liberalism manifests itself in various ways.
>
> Although the person concerned is clearly known to be in the wrong, yet because he is an old acquaintance, a fellow townsman, a school-friend, a bosom companion, a loved

one, an old colleague or a former subordinate, one does not argue with him on the basis of principle but lets things slide in order to maintain peace and friendship. Or one touches lightly upon the matter without finding a thorough solution, so as to maintain harmony all around. . . .

Liberalism stems from the selfishness of the petty bourgeoisie, which puts personal interest foremost and the interests of the revolution in the second place, thus giving rise to ideological, political, and organizational liberalism. . . .

Liberalism is a manifestation of opportunism and conflicts fundamentally with Marxism. It has a passive character and objectively has the effect of helping the enemy; thus the enemy welcomes its preservation in our midst. Such being its nature, there should be no place for it in the revolutionary ranks. (439–440)

Such was the view of Mao in the days of his early rectification campaigns to purge his Communist cadre of any bourgeois tendencies that might sap their militant spirit for class struggle.

After the close of the Cultural Revolution, followed by the death of Mao, the demise of the so-called Gang of Four, and the rise to leadership of Deng Xiaoping and Jiang Zemin, the situation changed substantially. It has no longer been dominated by Mao's insistence on class struggle as the defining element in revolutionary cultivation or by Liu Shaoqi's subordination of the individual to the group dynamics of the Communist Party. Emphasis is still put on the leadership of the party, but it is a party seen primarily as the guarantor of political stability and of the order needed to promote economic development.

The concerns expressed by Liang Qichao a century ago about the people's need to become citizens—how those who had not known anything but subjecthood under an imperial state could become full-fledged participants in a body politic—are still largely unaddressed. The "body-politic" is just the Communist Party and its members; everyone else is free to make a living or better, make a fortune (as Deng legitimized the business of becoming rich). Simply to participate in economic success is the idea, not to become politically active.

It is true, nonetheless, that anyone who visits a bookstore in China today sees a variety of literature, suggesting that the reading public at least has access to a wide range of ideas that would never have been tolerated under Mao, and on a person-to-person level there is little restraint on freedom of expression. Thus there is some room for discussion of public issues, in education and research institutions, professional organizations, and certain publications, the limits on which may vary according to local circumstances. This allows for far greater intellectual diversity than under Mao. It does not allow, however, for freedom of assembly or for organizations engaged in public advocacy unless they are registered with and subject to the control of the state administration.

In the present situation, after the liberalization of the economy under Deng, Jiang, and Hu Jintao, and the new admission of capitalists to membership in the Communist Party, some Western observers optimistically assume that capitalists will exert some liberal leavening effect on the party. The party leadership, however, seems to be convinced that capitalist liberals can be coopted to serve the party. Since in fact capitalists have no political organization of their own to advance more liberal goals, it is quite possible that the power of the state, still monopolized by the

Communist Party, will continue to curb any potential opposition and demonstrate the same repressive power as imperial regimes in the past. At this point there is more evidence of the will of the party to defend itself than there is of any organized opposition to liberalize it.

Meanwhile, apart from the immediate policy direction given by the party, a profound ideological vacuum has succeeded the collapse of Marx-Leninism both in China and worldwide. Accompanying it is an endemic moral crisis consequent on the lapse of the old self-sacrificing revolutionary morality, and the corruption of the body politic through the collusion of party members with the new capitalists and each other. The spectacle which the government often makes of the more obvious or politically vulnerable cases of corruption does little to remedy things. In a closed society it is always more difficult to detect and expose corruption than in an open one.

Under Deng Xiaoping and Jiang Zemin, the Rule of Law has been emphasized not only as a corrective to the excesses of the Mao Zedong era but as a check on corruption and to provide legal security for business enterprises. But rather than set too much store by the Rule of Law, Jiang also called for the Rule of Virtue, a move that seemed to echo the traditional view of the Confucians that personal virtue took precedence over law because the proper and fair enforcement of law depended on the conduct of the ruler and his officials. In Jiang's case, however, there is a question whether the slogan of Rule by Virtue does anything more than protect the superior authority of the Communist Party, as if it embodied superior political virtue by virtue of its revolutionary mandate. So far there is nothing to indicate that Jiang or his successors have in mind a systematic program of moral rectification and education by which the party would validate its claim to superior virtue—little more, so far, than show trials for the most egregious cases of corruption.

No doubt it is the awareness of widely prevalent corruption and a pervasive sense of moral crisis that has led some members of the postrevolutionary establishment to think of tradition as a source of remediation and to invoke such phrases as the Rule of Virtue. Chinese tradition is multiplex, however, and if a largely traditional cult like the Falun Gong—with its quasi-military discipline and organization—seems unamenable to party or state control, it is understandable that the regime might favor a more civil tradition like Confucianism to provide the Chinese content for a Chinese socialism. Thus it has sanctioned a Confucian Association to promote scholarly discussion of the subject, and traditional observances of rituals like the celebration of Confucius' birthday.

Nothing of this sort is likely to have any general effect on the Chinese people as a whole unless it partakes of a much wider educational effort. The question then becomes: on what level and of what sort? It is understandable that the establishment would favor a conservative brand of Confucianism, and indeed the Confucian Association identifies Harmony—political and social—rather than the Mencian challenge to authority, as the essence of the Chinese and Confucian tradition. As Gu Mu, a member of the Politburo at the time, said in a keynote speech at the 1989 celebration in Beijing of Confucius' 2540th anniversary celebration (a speech endorsed by Jiang Zemin):

As is known to all, the idea of harmony is an important component of the Chinese traditional culture. As early as the last years of the West Zhou dynasty three thousand years ago, ancient scholars elucidated the brilliant idea of "harmony making for prosperity." Later Confucius and the Confucian school put forward the proposition of "harmony above all" and established theories on the coordination of interpersonal relations, the protection of the natural environment, and the maintenance of ecological balance. These thoughts not only made positive contributions to the prosperity of ancient Chinese society but also have profound practical significance for the survival and development of mankind today. (582–583)

Since that time there have been celebratory rituals at shrines sacred to Confucius and considerable scholarly research on the history of Confucianism, but relatively little of this has found its way into the standard educational curriculum, let alone the political discourse. When the president of a major university in the south, sympathetic to Confucianism, wanted to include more of its teachings in the required curriculum for all students, he had difficulty substituting it for the standard Marx-Leninist-Maoist readings, but since local and regional universities and research institutions were allowed a little leeway in the promotion of local culture, he found a way to include Confucian readings in a local history course celebrating the adjacent site and tradition of a venerable Confucian academy.

In this way the Confucian record survives to some degree, but whether it will regain a vital role in China's education or political culture remains questionable—a question now complicated by the need for it to be seen not just as representing Chinese tradition but also as fitting into the public cultural setting of twenty-first century civilization. Thus it becomes a question also of how Confucianism is to be understood in relation to, first, its neighboring Confucian cultures in Korea, Japan, Taiwan, and Vietnam, and then to other world cultures that, in the last two centuries at least, have begun their own acquaintance with, and assimilation of, Confucianism.

In the context of this book, and in the perspective of an increasingly globalized education, if Confucianism, as representing the Chinese civil tradition, is to meet the challenge cited in the preface, the effort will require more than a return to the Chinese classics and a critical reengagement with tradition—necessary though these are. It will also mean an encounter with the seminal works of other major world traditions that speak to many of the same perennial issues.

This is a daunting challenge in itself, no matter how early the process starts or how long it goes on. What complicates the educational challenge still further is the need to go on from this first reading of the classics to a consideration of how the values discovered therein have been subjected to historical contestation and adaptation. To do this latter requires some discussion and continuing dialogue on key topics, as we have tried to do here.

Our choice of focus on nobility and civility responds to one immediate challenge of the present world situation—the threat of terrorism, conducted by highly committed leaders and perpetrated by dedicated followers. It is easy enough to lament the loss of civility which this betrays and betokens, and to pray piously for the restoration of peace. But the challenge thrown down by suicide bombers is more compelling. Though some observers may be inclined to dismiss these simply as fanatics, more thoughtful people feel impelled to look further into their motivations, or, for instance, in some schools decide to read the Qur'an for the first time or even take a crash course in Islam.

Any serious education should prepare one to understand the ultimate claims made not only by Muslim suicide bombers but also by their Hindu and Buddhist counterparts, as well as the Japanese samurai warriors or the suicide pilots Mishima Yukio wrote about. It is a lot to do, but this book tries to make a start at sorting out some of the key civilizational issues.

From this learning process we may hope to understand the appeal of different concepts of nobility as shared human ideals, the special attractiveness and lurking dangers these can hold for extreme forms of communalism and nationalism, and the civilities that in the longer run have helped to contain these dangers. On this basis we may also realize that there need be no inevitable clash of civilizations from irreducible cultural antagonisms but that from these diverse cultural and social traditions resources can be drawn on to cope with the challenges of environmental degradation, unrestrained economic competition, vicious political chauvinisms, and, more fundamentally, the deeper moral collapse and cultural despair that threaten world civilization in the twenty-first century.

Epilogue

At the start of this book we chose ("we" including the reader who has gone along with me this far) to start not with a preconceived definition of our themes of nobility and civility, but to engage in an open-ended exploration of what these concepts might have meant in different world traditions. In my case it was natural to start with the Confucians and the ways in which they projected a civil society governed by humane values, based primarily in a family ethic but opening up to the larger perspectives of a literate, urbane culture identified with the term *wen*—which distinguished a nonviolent, noncoercive civility from the martial values and virtues identified with the term *wu*.

In the longer term and from the East Asian perspective the martial values still counted, especially in the Japanese *bushidō* adaptation of the Confucian ethic, but for the most part the Confucians gave priority to the more benign and gentle qualities in which Confucius and the sage-kings were enshrined. Confucius himself, besides being canonized as "the sage" or "ultimate sage" *(chi sheng)*, was called the "king of civility spread abroad" *(wen-xuan wang)*. Among the founders of the Zhou Dynasty Confucians recognized both a warrior king (King Wu) and a civil king (King Wen), but it was the latter whose moral virtues were held up, in the classic "Ode to King Wen," for emulation by the educated ruling class.

The inclusion of odes in the Confucian canon is indicative of the high place literature had in both the earlier and the later, codified tradition and reminds us that aesthetic values were a significant component of this civil tradition. Moreover, the importance of ritual, again in both the classic and the later, more developed tradition, represented a significant balancing of the moral and rational tendencies by aesthetic proclivities.

Early in the *Analects* the tension between these competing but also complementary values was reflected in a passage wherein Confucius is quoted as assigning a first priority to the family ethic and only a secondary derivative status to polite letters (*Analects* 1:6). Nevertheless this aesthetic dimension played a prominent part in the cultural diffusion of Confucianism down through the ages, especially in the form of poetry and painting as major vehicles for the expression of Confucian values and their dissemination, first in East Asia and then in the larger world.

The importance of the polite arts in Confucianism—which brings out one feature of the *junzi* as the cultured gentleman (otherwise distinguished for the nobility of his moral character)—also points to a cultural bridge between this tradition and neighboring ones. Emulation of the Confucian ideal is actually realized in the aesthetic gentility of the Heian aristocracy (exemplified by Prince Genji as representative of a courtliness that formally acknowledges Confucian culture but is much more given to the aesthetic and emotional side of the native Japanese tradition). But this aesthetic dimension also has a recognizable affinity to the "courtliness" of the man-about-town whose urbanity is celebrated in the Indian *Kama Sutra*—a courtliness and gentility that, as associated with townspeople, stands in some contrast with the moral nobility of King Rama as an exercise of restraint on the part of the ruling elite. Examination of these ideals reveals both the commonalities and diversities within and among Asian traditions— enough commonalities so that one could conceive of shared Asian values even though one recognizes that historically there was little cross-fertilization between, say, Confucianism and Hinduism. Had the classics of the two traditions been shared, their adherents would have recognized in Rama many of the civil virtues with which they endowed the Confucian noble man, and in the idealized Confucian sage-kings seen many of the restraints on the exercise of power illustrated in Indian epics like the *Ramayana* and *Mahabharata* or the classic drama *Shakuntala*.

Among the commonalities (embedded of course in different cultural and historical contexts) are problematic features as well—problematic in that they represent similar conflicts with and challenges to classic values. We have seen how Buddhism appeared as a challenge to a Brahmanical religion regarded as too much bound up with caste and family values, offering a spirituality that claimed to transcend these social limitations. And although Mahayana Buddhism made its peace with both social and political institutions through its extensive repertoire of expedient means, something of its radical critique of established culture survived in all those forms of the Mahayana that still saw such accommodations as ultimately "empty."

All this is cast still in the language of ideal traditional values—conflicting and conflicted though they were historically. For our purposes here it is enough to recognize that our approach to these contested values is possible even in the reading of the classic texts and canonical scriptures themselves, to say nothing of the changing historical circumstances that pose their own challenge to tradition. As we extend the reading of the classics to the reading of later texts in the same or merging traditions, we can recognize two main features of the evolving traditions themselves. One is that the classics have already commanded attention within their own culture because they have taken up central ground and have staked out axial positions from which later writers and thinkers can get their bearings, even if only to take issue with earlier formulations. The other point is that the axial formulations themselves are pivotal and multifaceted enough so that they afford the grounds for their own internal contestation and self-criticism, as well as the grounds for responding to the challenge of competing traditions.

This is a basic point at a time when political conflicts and culture wars incline some people to believe in the inevitable clash of civilizations or the basic incompatibility of different cultures. There is enough violence in the twenty-first century to persuade one that the twentieth century's liberal assumptions of "one world" as a natural and rational development are being shaken to the ground. But before we conclude that superior force is the only way to resolve such inherent conflicts we owe it to ourselves to make another, more determined effort to understand how the multivariate and multivalent resources available within these traditions afford the means for a meaningful discourse to take place on each other's terms.

Recall the case in which recourse was had to such discourse in order to resolve cultural dilemmas in the encounter between Chinese and Japanese traditions—Shōtoku's
resort to the native tradition of consultation and consensus
formation as a practical means of resolving contradictions
between the basic assumptions of Buddhism and Confucianism. This solution of Shōtoku's was successful up to a
point in mediating contending interests and forces, but its
pragmatic flexibility worked better at reconciling private interests and feelings than it did at articulating definite values that could sustain public discourse to advance and uphold the common good. Thus in early modern and modern
times Japan has been seeking agreement on conscious values, rational choices, and policies that go beyond intimate
feelings and instincts. These latter, at best, can only hold
together local communities on the basis of parochial loyalties—as witness the failure of twentieth-century ultra-
nationalists who tried to graft feudal loyalties into a new
modern ideology.

This is not, however, a dilemma only for the Japanese or
appearing only in a Japanese guise. In one way or another
we all face it. A contrasting formulation of it in what might
be thought characteristically Western terms is found in a
recent essay by Ira Katznelson, the title of which, "Evil and
Politics," is evocative of the moral dilemmas of contemporary liberals in dealing with the problem of evil palpably at
large and on the loose in a world of violence and terror.

Both liberalism and the Enlightenment within it
nestles advance a philosophical anthropology of rational ac-
tors and rational action, insisting that human agents develop the capacity to deliberate, choose, and achieve sensi-

ble goals. In their effort to cultivate such rational citizens, liberal regimes in the past have all too often imposed various limits, drawing boundaries that stunt the capacities of individuals based on their religion, race, gender, literacy, criminality, or colonized status. But after centuries of struggle about the dimensions of freedom, enlightened political liberalism today acknowledges *no* legitimate barriers to reason, hence no legitimate ascriptive barriers to liberal inclusion and liberal citizenship.

The result is a deep paradox. The global appeal of an enlightened liberalism cannot help but jeopardize the local attachments, the historical particularities—the human plurality—that constitute its most important rationale.

Here, then, lies liberalism's most basic current conundrum: How to broaden its endowments in order to protect and nourish heterogeneity while coping with its perils.[1]

The liberalism Katznelson is talking about is not, I think, the Whig liberalism of the nineteenth century or some twentieth-century political ideology, but rather a longer-term view that is informed by a perennial humanistic tradition—more like what the classicist Gilbert Murray called "liberality," a virtue of the ancients still recognizable by fin-de-siècle British gentlemen as an attribute of classic nobility. A similar view was expressed by Mark Van Doren when he spoke of the need for the liberal imagination to deal with the challenges of multiculturalism in the mid-twentieth century:

Imagination always has work to do, whether in single minds or in the general will. . . . Without it, for instance, the West can come to no conclusions about the East which war and fate are rapidly making a necessary object of its knowledge. Statistics and surveys of the East will not produce what an

image can produce: an image of difference, so that no gross
offenses are committed against the human fact of strangeness, and an image of similarity, even of identity, so that
nothing homely is forgotten.[2]

Van Doren's language, from an age somewhat more optimistic than ours, may be less fraught with the sense of peril
manifest in Katznelson's essay, but it is no less mindful of
the challenge for us in trying to cope with the paradoxical
"human fact of strangeness" (the heterogeneity Katznelson
seeks to nourish), or in possibly forgetting what is "homely"
—making ourselves at home with, or making room for, others' most simple and intimate but also most strongly held
beliefs (Katznelson's "local attachments").

Any multicultural learning should start by showing respect
for the way each tradition has defined itself—how its own
canon formation has established its own value criteria by
dialogue among its recognized authorities, including the
contestation that has gone on within the parameters of
that discourse. This establishes a context within which any
given work, theme, or issue may be understood, and provides the grounds or framework for further comparative
discussion of similarities and differences among them.

Within each major tradition this dialogue has taken
place through a process of constant, repeated cross-refer-
encing and back-referencing, internal to the tradition and
largely independent of external involvement except to the
extent that, from at least the seventeenth century onwards,
writers in the West, great and not so great, have confirmed
for themselves what important writers in the Islamic, Indian, Chinese, and Japanese traditions have long held in

esteem. It is of crucial importance, however, that enough of the original discourse be reproduced so that this internal dialogue can be recognized and meaningfully evaluated by the reader.

The present book illustrates such an approach. Among the many themes that are worth exploring, one in particular stands out as having a close relevance to the issues of human rights and civil society: the status of the individual or person.

One still hears, all too often, statements by supposedly educated persons and even prominent intellectuals that the dignity of the individual is a peculiarly Western or Judeo-Christian idea and that people who do not recognize it cannot be expected to respect human rights. Conversely, those who claim to speak for Asian communitarian ideals charge concepts of human rights with being too individualistic, too Western, and too heedless of the claims that the community or state may make on the individual. In reality most Asian religions and philosophies, from the dawn of civilizations, have exhibited a self-awareness and a consciousness of individual responsibility predicated on a high evaluation of the human potential—variously expressed in language that affirms this value in relation to the different ends of life that might be served by, or serve, individuals. In Confucian terms this could be the concept of personhood —the realizing through self-cultivation of a fully formed and developed person. Proper forms of respect to be shown such persons were often defined in accordance with their status, but no one stood so low that his autonomy, based on his inherent human nature, should not be respected (*Analects* 2:3, 9:25).

One could of course dwell on the differentiated aspects

of Confucian ritual decorum as contrasted with the radical autonomy asserted by some modern libertarian movements, but anyone who believes in a common humanity underlying human rights could, I think, go along with what the Japanese Confucian Nakamura Masanao has said above about unities and continuities in the midst of cultural differences: "As far as individual morality is concerned, regardless of past and present, East or West, the main principle is the one thing of self-governance. . . . This is the central concern of the independent self and is the source of the principle of freedom" (ch. 8).

The kind of liberal learning we need to incorporate in education will serve its purpose if it produces citizens who are not only less culture-bound (that is, not just exposed to a shapeless cultural diversity), but equipped to deal with actual conflict. As an illustration of what multicultural exposure can do to promote conflict resolution and enhance civil discourse, we may recall the experience at the United Nations in the post-World War II years, when the Universal Declaration of Human Rights (1948) was being drafted. It happened that among the diplomats represented there were Chinese who had been graduate students of John Dewey at Columbia. Though not untypical of the New Culture generation in China of the 1910s and 1920s, often better educated in Western subjects than in Chinese, the alienation some of them felt from Confucian tradition was offset by Dewey's own sympathetic interest in Confucianism, which turned them back to the study of Chinese philosophy or at least to a more informed awareness and appreciation of it. As a result, when Chinese of this sort participated in the drafting of the Universal Declaration at the U.N., they saw to it that the language used was inclusive enough to allow for the reading of its provisions in a larger Confucian, humanist, perspective.

A consequence of this adjustment was a wide acceptance and adoption of the Declaration by Asian nations as well as Western. It is true that the actual observance of its provisions has left much to be desired, and among spokesmen for authoritarian rule in East and South Asia these ostensibly universal human rights formulations have often been belittled as too Western. But the formal adoption of the Universal Declaration by most states, even if only as a matter of lip-service, has nevertheless established a standard by which actual practice can be measured and judged. Thus even the relatively modest contribution of persons whose education bridges two or more cultures, could make a difference in gradually advancing civil discourse and a multicultural or intercultural civility. This may represent only a modest advance and perhaps be too slow to overtake the impassioned violence breaking out all over the twenty-first century world, but education genuinely respectful of human dignity, shared in all its manifest diversity, calls for such patient and determined effort from us all.

The classical Confucian philosopher Xunzi said long ago, in arguing the case for purposive learning as essential to the survival of civilized life, that it calls for a "dogged will" and "dull and determined effort"[3] to carry what Confucius had called "the burden of humaneness" down the long road of life.

Notes

1. Confucius' Noble Person

1. Yoshino Sakuzō, *Minpon shugiron*, 4–6; trans. A. Tiedemann, *SJT,* 218–219.
2. de Bary, Bloom, *SCT* I, 29.
3. The quotation is from an unknown work purporting to describe the government of the Xia dynasty in high antiquity. It was later incorporated into the short text titled "Yin zheng," one of the spurious sections of the *Classic of Documents* that were put together in the third century CE.
4. Watson, *The Tso chuan*, xv–xvi.
5. *Shiji* (BNB) 87:6b-7a; Watson, in *SCT* I, 209–210.

2. The Noble Paths of Buddha and Rama

1. *The Dhammapada,* trans. Carter and Palihawadana, 239. All subsequent citations are to this edition and are henceforth identified by page numbers in the text.
2. Ling, *The Buddha's Philosophy of Man*, 100–113 (hereafter citations are by page number in the text).
3. de Bary, ed., *The Buddhist Tradition*, 54 (hereafter citations are by page number in the text).
4. Swearer, *The Buddhist World of Southeast Asia*, 66–92 (hereafter citations are by page number in the text).
5. See Van Doren, *The Noble Voice*.
6. *The Rāmāyana of Valmiki*, Goldman, gen. ed.; vol. 2, *Ayodhyakanda*, trans. Sheldon Pollock, 299–301.

7. *The Kama Sutra of Vatsyayana,* trans. Burton, 76. Literally, a "man of city or town." Compare "man about town" in *Kamasutra,* trans. Doniger and Kukar, 17.
8. Doniger, 19; Burton, 76.
9. Burton, 78–79; Doniger, 20.
10. *The Sukraniti,* trans. Sarkar, 114–126 (hereafter citations are by page number in the text).
11. Tiruvalluvar, *The Kural,* 75 (hereafter citations are by page number in the text).
12. Gandhi, *Hind Swaraj,* 31–81 (hereafter citations are by page number in the text).

3. Buddhist Spirituality and Chinese Civility

1. *SCT* I, 427–428.
2. Ibid.
3. *The Vimalakirti Sutra,* trans. Watson, 110.
4. *Lotus Sutra,* trans. Watson, 187–188; *SCT* I, 453–454.
5. Paul Groner, "The *Lotus Sutra* and Saicho's Interpretation of the Realization of Buddhahood with This Very Body," in Tanabe, *The Lotus Sutra in Japanese Culture,* 61.
6. Peach, "Social Responsibility, . . . in the *Lotus Sutra,*" 50n1.
7. Jan Yunhua, "Chinese Buddhism in Ta-tu," in de Bary, Hoklam Chan, eds., *Yuan Thought,* 387–388.
8. Ibid.
9. *SCT* I, 476–477; trans. and commentary by Charles D. Orzech.
10. Ibid., 477.
11. Ibid., 478.
12. See Jinhua Chen, "More Than a Philosopher: Fazang (643–712) as a Politician and Miracle Worker," in *History of Religions,* v. 42, n. 4 (May 2003), pp. 320–358.

4. Shōtoku's Constitution and the Civil Order in Early Japan

1. de Bary et al., eds., *SJT* I, 51–53.
2. de Bary, ed., *The Buddhist Tradition,* 310–311.
3. Ibid., 313.
4. See Ryuichi Abe, *The Weaving of Mantra,* 326–333.
5. Ibid., 334.

5.   Chrysanthemum and Sword Revisited

1. The *Manyōshū*, 10.
2. See Murasaki, *The Tale of Genji*, 501–502.
3. Morris, *The World of the Shining Prince*, 106.
4. Sei Shōnagon, *The Pillow Book*, 127–129.
5. See Borgen, *Sugawara no Michizane*, 175–176, 275, 283.
6. Benedict, *The Chrysanthemum and the Sword*, 295–296.
7. Jeffrey Mass, in Hall and Mass, *Medieval Japan*, 248.
8. *SJT* I, 279–280; trans. adapted from McCullough, *Tale of the Heike*, 316–317.
9. *Sarugaku* is a theatrical form from which Noh is derived. As used here, *sarugaku* may mean Noh.
10. *SJT* I, 428; adapted from trans. of Paul Varley.
11. *SJT* I, pp. 231, 235.
12. Dobbins, *Jōdo Shinshū*.
13. Yamamoto, *Hagakure*, in *NST* v. 26: 2, 113, 195; adapted from trans. by Barry Steben in *SJT* II.
14. *SJT* I, 448; adapted from trans. by J. S. A. Elisonas.
15. *SJT* II, trans. by W. J. Boot.
16. Hayashi Razan, *Bakufu mondō*, *NST* 28, 207–208; adapted from trans. by W. J. Boot in *SJT* II.

6.   The New Leadership and Civil Society in Song China

1. Han Yü, "On the Way," adapted from trans. by Charles Hartman in *SCT* I, 570–571 (henceforth cited by page number in the text).
2. *SCT* I, 767–770.
3. "Counsels of the Great Yu," *Classic of Documents*, trans. by James Legge, 3:61.
4. *SCT* I, 732–733 (henceforth cited by page number in the text).
5. See de Bary and Haboush, eds., *The Rise of Neo-Confucianism in Korea*, 323–348; and *Sources of Korean Tradition* II, ch. 24.

7.   Civil and Military in Tokugawa Japan

1. See Sakai Tadao in de Bary and Haboush, eds., *Rise of Neo-Confucianism in Korea*, 343–344.
2. See *SCT* I, 767–770.
3. Muro Kyūsō, *Rikuyu engi taii*, 584–588; trans. by de Bary in *SJT* II, Ch. 26.

4. Ramseyer, *House Codes*, 227–230.
5. Fujiwara Seika, *Seika Sensei bunshū*, in *NST* 28, 88–90. Trans. adapted from W. J. Boot in *SJT* II, ch. 21.
6. Han Xin was a famous general who served Liu Bang, the first emperor of the Han; Xiang Yu was the great Chu general who fought Liu Bang for the Chinese empire.
7. Nakae Tōju, *Okina mondō*, in *NST* 29, 65, 115; trans. Barry Steben in *SJT* II, ch. 22.
8. Keene, *Four Major Plays of Chikamatsu*, 131.
9. That is, Japan, east of the central Kingdom, China. Korean Confucians also referred to their country as "eastern" in relation to China.
10. *SJT* II, ch. 31.
11. Fukuzawa Yukichi, *Encouragement of Learning*, 65–66; trans. adapted from Dilworth and Hirano, 37–38.
12. The first reference is to Zhu Xi's preface to the *Great Learning* (see *SCT* I, 722–724). The second is to Zhu's *Elementary Learning* (see *SCT* I, 803–804). Shōnan does not disagree with Zhu Xi but only with later Neo-Confucians who fail to fulfill these aims.
13. Yokoi Shōnan, *Kokuze sanron*, in *NST* 44, 439–465.

8. Citizen and Subject in Modern Japan

1. Fukuzawa Yukichi, *An Outline of a Theory of Civilization*, 13–15, 35 (hereafter cited by page number in the text).
2. See *Mencius* 7A:15.
3. Part of the "sixteen-character formula" of Zhu Xi.
4. A reference to Zhu Xi's explanation of the sixteen-character formula in his preface to the *Mean:* "If one applies oneself to this without any interruption, making sure that the mind of the Way is the master of one's self and that the human mind always listens to its commands, then the precariousness and insecurity will yield to peace and security, and what is subtle and barely perceptible will become clearly manifest." See *SCT* I, 732–733.
5. *Analects* 6:9.
6. The *Mean*, Section 8.
7. Nakamura, "Kokin tōzai itchi," 326–333.
8. Kikuchi Dairoku, *Japanese Education*, 646.
9. Gluck, *Japan's Modern Myths*, 129–130.
10. See *SJT,* 277–278 (Fundamentals of Our National Polity).

11. Trans. adapted from Dilworth et al., eds., *Sourcebook for Modern Japanese Philosophy,* 279–287.
12. *SJT,* 527–528 (hereafter cited by page number in the text).
13. Yamamoto, *Hagakure,* in *NST* v. 26, pt. 1, nos. 2, 113, 195; trans. adapted from Barry Steben in *SJT* I, ch. 13; *SJT* II, ch. 31.
14. Maruyama, "8/15 and 5/19" in *Chūō kōron,* August 1960, p. 51; cf. Andrew Gordon in *SJT* II, 1805–06.
15. *Mishima Yukio hyōron zenshū,* 227–228 (hereafter cited by page number in the text).

9.   "The People Renewed" in Twentieth-Century China

1. See de Bary, *Waiting for the Dawn.*
2. de Bary et al., eds., *SCT* II, 289–291 (hereafter cited by page number in the text).
3. Readers of this essay will recall how Fujiwara Seika at the turn of the sixteenth/seventeenth century dealt with trading relations by extending the value of trustworthiness characteristic of the friend-to-friend relationship. Liang Shuming apparently feels that this is insufficient to express the relationships of member to group in a way that would fulfill Zhu Xi's and Wang Yangming's sense of community responsibility.
4. Trans. by Catherine Lynch in *SCT* II, 382–385.
5. These were the virtues of Confucius, as described by one of the disciples. (Note in the original.)
6. A disciple of Confucius. (Note in the original.)
7. *The Great Learning* is said to be "a Book handed down by the Confucian school, which forms the gate by which beginners enter into virtue." (Note in the original.)

Epilogue

1. Katznelson, "Evil and Politics," 9–10.
2. Van Doren, *Liberal Education,* 127. Quoted in de Bary and Bloom, *Approaches to the Asian Classics,* 20.
3. *Hsun Tzu,* 20.

Works Cited

Abe, Ryūichi. 1999. *The Weaving of Mantra*. New York: Columbia University Press.

Benedict, Ruth. 1946. *The Chrysanthemum and the Sword*. New York: Houghton Mifflin.

Borgen, Robert. 1986. *Sugawara no Michizane and the Early Heian Court*. Cambridge, Mass.: Harvard University Press.

Ch'oe, Yongho, W. T. de Bary, and Peter Lee, eds. 2000. *Sources of Korean Tradition II*. New York: Columbia University Press.

Classic of Documents. 1893–1895. Trans. James Legge. In *The Chinese Classics* (trans. James Legge). Oxford: Clarendon Press.

de Bary, Wm. Theodore. 1998. *Asian Values and Human Rights*. Cambridge: Harvard University Press.

——— 1993. *Waiting for the Dawn*. New York: Columbia University Press.

——— ed. 1969. *The Buddhist Tradition*. New York: Random House.

——— and Irene Bloom. 1990. *Approaches to the Asian Classics*. New York: Columbia University Press.

——— and Irene Bloom, eds. 1999. *Sources of Chinese Tradition*, 2nd. ed., v. I (abbrev. in the notes as *SCT* I). New York: Columbia University Press.

——— and Hoklam Chan, eds. 1982. *Yuan Thought*. New York: Columbia University Press.

——— and JaHyun Haboush, eds. 1985. *The Rise of Neo-Confucianism in Korea*. New York: Columbia University Press.

———, et al., eds. 1999. *Sources of Chinese Tradition*, 2nd ed., v. II (abbrev. in the notes as *SCT* II). New York: Columbia University Press.

————, et al., eds. 1958. *Sources of Japanese Tradition,* 1st ed. (abbrev. in the notes as *SJT*). New York: Columbia University Press.

————, et al., eds. 2001. *Sources of Japanese Tradition,* 2nd ed. v. I (abbrev. in the notes as *SJT* I). New York: Columbia University Press.

————. et al., eds. 2004, forthcoming. *Sources of Japanese Tradition,* 2nd. ed. v. II (abbrev. in the notes as SJT II). New York: Columbia University Press.

The Dhammapada (4th c. BCE–4th c. CE). 1987. Trans. John Ross Carter and Mahinda Palihawadana. New York: Oxford University Press.

Dilworth, David, et al., eds. 1998. *Sourcebook for Modern Japanese Philosophy.* Westport, CT: Greenwood Press.

Dobbins, James. 1989. *Jōdo Shinshū, Shin Buddhism in Medieval Japan.* Bloomington: Indiana University Press

Fujiwara Seika. 1958–1978. *Fujiwara Seika Sensei bunshū* (Collected Works of Fujiwara Seika). In *Nihon shisō taikei* 28 (series abbrev. in the notes as *NST*). Tokyo: Iwanami shoten.

Fukuzawa Yukichi. 1969. *An Encouragement of Learning.* Trans. David Dilworth and Umeyo Hirano. Tokyo: Sophia University Press.

———— 1973. *An Outline of a Theory of Civilization.* Trans. David Dilworth and G. Cameron Hurst. Tokyo: Sophia University Press.

Gandhi, Mohandas. 1938. *Hind Swaraj or Indian Home Rule.* Ahmedabad: Narajivan Publishing House.

Gluck, Carol. 1985. *Japan's Modern Myths.* Princeton: Princeton University Press.

Hall, John Whitney and Jeffrey Mass. 1974. *Medieval Japan.* Stanford: Stanford University Press.

Hayashi Razan. 1978 (17th c.). *Bakufu mondō, Razan sensei bunshū* (Answers to Questions of the Bakufu). *Nihon shisō taikei* 28. Tokyo: Iwanami shoten.

Hsun Tzu. 1967. Trans. Burton Watson. New York: Columbia University Press.

The Kama Sutra of Vatsyayana. 1962. Trans. Sir Richard Burton. New York: Dutton.

Kamasutra. 2002. Trans. Wendy Doniger and Sudhir Kukar. New York: Oxford University Press.

Katznelson, Ira. 2002. "Evil and Politics," *Daedalus*, v. 13, n. 1 (Winter). Cambridge, Mass.: American Academy of Arts and Sciences.

Keene, Donald. 1967. *Essays in Idleness. The Tsurezuregusa of Kenkō* (1331). New York: Columbia University Press.

——— 1961. *Four Major Plays of Chikamatsu*. New York: Columbia University Press.

Kikuchi, Dairoku. 1909. *Japanese Education*. London: J. Murray.

Ling, Trevor. 1981. *The Buddha's Philosophy of Man*. London: J. M. Dent and Sons.

Lotus Sutra. 1993. Trans. Burton Watson. New York: Columbia University Press.

The Manyōshū. 1941. (Collection of Ten Thousand Pages, 8th cent.) Ed. Nippon gakujutsu shinkōkai. Chicago: University of Chicago Press.

Maruyama Masao. 1960. "8/15 and 5/19," article in *Chūō kōron*, August. Tokyo: Chūō Kōronsha.

McCullough, Helen Craig. 1988. *Tale of the Heike*. Stanford: Stanford University Press.

Mishima Yukio. 1989. *Mishima Yukio hyōron zenshū* (Collected Essays of Mishima Yukio), v. 3. Tokyo: Shinchōsha.

Morris, Ivan. 1964. *The World of the Shining Prince*. New York: Knopf.

[Lady] Murasaki Shikibu. 1935. *The Tale of Genji*. Trans. Arthur Waley. New York: Literary Guild.

Muro Kyūsō. 1910–22. *Rikuyu engi taii, Nihon kyōiku bunko*. Kankai I. Tokyo: Dōbunkan.

Nakae Tōju. 1964. *Okina mondō*. In *Nihon shisō taikei*, v. 29. Tokyo: Iwanami.

Nakamura, Keiu (Masano). 1967 (orig. 1890). "Kokin tōzai itchi dōtoku no setsu" (Past-Present, East-West: One Morality), in *Tōkyō Gakushikaiin zasshi*, April 14, 1890. In Ōkubo Toshiaki, *Meiji keimō shisō shū* (Enlightenment Thought in the Meiji Period), v. 3 of *Meiji bungaku zenshū* (Collected Writings of Meiji Literature). Tokyo: Chikuma shobō.

Nihon shisō taikei (abbrev. *NST*). 1958–1978. 67 vols. Tokyo: Iwanami shoten.

Peach, Linda Joy. 2002. "Social Responsibility, Sex Change, and Salvation: Gender Justice in the *Lotus Sutra.*" *Philosophy East and West,* v. 52. n. 1, January. Honolulu: University of Hawai'i Press.

The Rāmāyana of Valmiki. 1984. Gen. ed. Robert P. Goldman. Vol. 2, *Ayodhyakanda,* trans. Sheldon Pollock. Princeton: Princeton University Press.

Ramseyer, J. Mark. 1979. "House Codes of Tokugawa Merchants," *Monumenta Nipponica* 34. Tokyo: Sophia University.

Sei Shōnagon. 1967 (10th c.). *The Pillow Book.* Trans. Ivan Morris. New York: Columbia University Press.

Sima Qian. 1961. *Shiji.* Partial trans. Burton Watson, *Records of the Grand Historian,* 2 vols. New York: Columbia University Press.

The Sukraniti. 1975 (10th–16th c.). Trans. B. K. Sarkar. New Delhi: Orient Books.

Swearer, Donald K. 1995. *The Buddhist World of Southeast Asia.* Albany: SUNY Press.

Tanabe, George and Willa, eds. 1989. *The Lotus Sutra in Japanese Culture.* Honolulu: University of Hawai'i Press.

Tiruvalluvar. *The Kural.* 1991. Trans. P. S. Sundaram. London: Penguin.

Van Doren, Mark. 1943. *Liberal Education.* New York: Holt.

——— 1946. *The Noble Voice: A Study of the Great Poems.* New York: Holt.

The Vimalakirti Sutra. 1997. Trans. Burton Watson. New York: Columbia University Press.

Watson, Burton. 1989. *The Tso chuan: Selections from China's Oldest Narrative History.* New York: Columbia University Press.

Yamamoto Tsunetomo. 1958–1978 (18th c.). *Hagakure* (In the Shadow of Leaves). In *NST* v. 26. Tokyo: Iwanami shoten.

Yokoi Shōnan. 1958–1978 (orig. 1860). *Kokuze sanron* (Three Essays on National Policy). *NST* v. 44. Tokyo: Iwanami shoten.

Yoshino Sakuzō. 1946. *Minpon shugiron* (Democracy). Tokyo: Shinkigensha.

Zhu Xi. 1999 (12th c.). *Xiaoxue* (Elementary Learning). As excerpted in *SCT* I, 767–780.

Index